Re-engineering at Work

Second Edition

To the memory of my long-suffering mother

Wang Baozhen
(1932–1993)

who taught me more about forbearance and fortitude
than she could have imagined and, regretfully, never
lived to see the fruits of those efforts

and to my father

Luo Yanlong

who continues to teach me how to walk the talk

Re-engineering at Work

Second edition

Dr Michael Loh

Gower

Published by
Gower Publishing Limited
Gower House
Croft Road
Aldershot
Hampshire GU11 3HR
England

Gower
Old Post Road
Brookfield
Vermont 05036
USA

British Library Cataloguing in Publication Data

Loh, Michael, 1957–
    Re-engineering at work. – 2nd ed.
    1. Organizational change 2. Reengineering (Management)
    I. Title
    658.4'063

    ISBN 0 566 07941 0

Typeset in 10¹/₂ point Baskerville by Bournemouth Colour Press Ltd, and printed in Great Britain by Hartnolls, Bodmin.

Contents

List of Figures ix

Preface xi

Acknowledgements xxi

Part I: STEP ONE
Establishing the Change Imperative

Chapter 1   Positioning for Change   3

PART II: STEP TWO
Creating Vision and Targets

Chapter 2   Envisioning the Future   23

Chapter 3   Using the Balanced Scorecard   43

Chapter 4   Benchmarking Your Way
             to the Top!   51

Chapter 5   Operational Diagnosis
             Why We Work the Way We Do   63

Chapter 6   Behavioural Analysis
             The Touchy Feely Stuff   77

Chapter 7   Leadership and Power
             Who's Who in Your Organization 89

Chapter 8   A Fish Rots from the Head   101

Part III: STEP THREE
Redesigning, Building and Implementing

Chapter 9   Creativity
             *Going Where No One Has Gone
             Before*   111

Chapter 10   Re-engineering and Human
             Resources
             *The Minds Behind the Warm
             Bodies*   121

Chapter 11   Redesign
             Aiming for the Jugular   145

Chapter 12   Information Technology as an
             Enabler   153

Part IV: STEP FOUR
Sustaining Long-Term Results

Chapter 13   Perpetuation
             Now and For Ever More   163

Part V
Looking Ahead

Chapter 14   What Next?   177

Chapter 15   The Asian Way   187

Recommended Reading   197

Index   215

List of Personnel with Affiliations   223

Company List   225

List of Figures

2.1   How not to develop a vision   26

2.2   Marriott's vision   32

2.3   AIA's mission statement   32

2.4   Wuthelam's core values and objectives   33

2.5   Cathay Pacific's public statement of commitment   34

3.1   The Balanced Scorecard   45

6.1   Heart-beat study for Dow Corning, 1994   86

13.1   The change curve   170

Preface

I am championing what might be called a modest proposal to save organizations from ruin.

When people ask me what I do for a living, I tell them that I'm reversing the Industrial Revolution. And if this sounds just a tad ambitious, don't tell those blue-chip organizations in Asia, Europe and the United States that have hired people like me as consultants. Because the gospel we preach – re-engineering – is not only management's hottest new buzzword, but it really works.

The path to re-engineering was first paved by Toyota, the Japanese company which revolutionized production processes and delivery capabilities during the mid-1950s. With the 1973 oil embargo, other Japanese companies also learned their process-oriented concepts and began to convert to process-driven production. By 1983 the basic principles of the Toyota production system – what we now know as Just-In-Time (JIT) manufacturing – were well known in the executive suites of the largest companies in the West.

I'm not alone. Numerous consulting firms, from companies such as Booz Allen & Hamilton to KPMG Peat Marwick, Arthur D. Little to Gemini, are peddling, under one guise or another, re-engineering advice. For fees that can approach US$500 000 dollars a month, they will help you turn your company inside out while promising drastic cuts in processing costs, product defects and delivery time. Often the benefits sound almost too good to believe. A frequent promise is that re-engineering should lead to a hundredfold rather than a 100 per cent improvement.

Some companies that have used these consultants swear by re-engineering, saying its promise of massive rather than incremental change can greatly improve results. For others, however, the concept is the latest in a line of management fads, the successor to Total Quality Management – a programme of the 1980s that, many of its practitioners admit now, did not live up to its original expectations.

The nagging suspicion: a decade from now, people may be saying the same thing about re-engineering.

Re-engineering can be a hazy term, a concept that means different things to the different consulting firms using it to sell their services. It is also a grossly misused term.

The word was co-invented by former MIT professor of computer science Michael Hammer and it became popular in 1993 when his book *Re-engineering the*

Corporation, written with James Champy, was released (both were involved in re-engineering consulting but have gone separate ways since). Hammer said that the worse misuse of the word was when somebody referred to the replacing of office furniture as re-engineering.

Several seminars conducted in the Singapore region not long ago, many of them with the word 're-engineering' in their titles, had absolutely nothing to do with the subject. A *Newsweek* cover story on the subject exhibited extremely poor knowledge of it. The term is now applied to anything from restaurant menus to mothers-in-law, from an excuse to fire people to a buzzword for change.

Some experts say that re-engineering will eliminate between 1 million and 2.5 million jobs each year for the foreseeable future. This is not necessarily true. GE Fanuc Automation North America re-engineered without having to lay off workers. In fact, it has 3 per cent more workers than two years ago. The real point of this is longer-term growth on the revenue side. It's not so much getting rid of people. It's getting more out of people. What must be kept in mind is that re-engineering differs from downsizing. Rather than simply shrinking the current organization, re-engineering streamlines processes across organizational lines, eliminating hand-offs and producing radical, dramatic changes. Downsizing isn't re-engineering and I don't accept blame for the misappropriation of the term.

In some ways the term 're-engineering' is a misnomer. It implies that processes in organizations have been engineered in the first place. However, most processes are products of a complex series of deliberate decisions and informal evolution.

For me, re-engineering means radically changing the way work is done in an organization rather than improving existing processes by, say, automating them – paving the village tracks with asphalt.

A workable definition of re-engineering is 'a *multidisciplinary* approach to *implementing fundamental change* in the way work is performed *across the organization* with the goal of *dramatically improving* performance and stakeholder *value*'.

This was the definition used by Deloitte Touche Tohmatsu International when I was their principal consultant and partner-in-training.

Work processes haven't changed much since Adam Smith wrote the first chapter of his economic treatise *An*

Inquiry into The Wealth of Nations more than 200 years ago. In that chapter, dealing with the division of labour, Smith prescribed job specialization and hierarchical control as a way to achieve economies of scale and efficiency, thereby laying the foundation for modern mass production.

But in a world of tough international competition, demanding customers and rapid change, this traditional bureaucratic structure doesn't work: work, done traditionally, results in costly delays and complications threatening the competitiveness of organizations all over the world.

Companies, instead of installing computer systems to automate existing processes, should consider tearing down those processes and starting from scratch – straighten rather than merely pave the village tracks.

I see my role mainly as a barnstorming agenda-setter for modern business who leaves the details of implementing re-engineering in particular companies to their staff whom I will train.

Chief executive officers (CEOs) today are desperate for new paradigms. There is a despair that they cannot change their organizations quickly enough to cope with the tremendous growth. Having learned that relentless cost reduction can't go on for ever and doesn't reach the root problems anyway, members of upper management are willing to bet on something that will reshape as well as trim down their companies and achieve massive increases in profitability. The trouble is that mediocre consultants are everywhere – and if an axe is all you have, you'll regard every problem as a tree. I have seen consultants recommending job evaluation when what their client needs is a massive organizational overhaul.

None of the management fads of the last two decades has been effective in saving organizations from ruin: not one-minute managing; not 'unleashing one's hidden power'; not lateral thinking; not manloading or crewing; not customer service (preaching customer service in 'come-to-Jesus' boot camps without equipping people with infrastructures to work with is nothing more than mental masturbation); not even *excellence* – most of the companies showcased in the Peters and Waterman book *In Search of Excellence* have managed themselves to the brink of collapse.

Since 1993 ISO 9000 has been the hot topic, especially in Asia. Is it what it is made out to be?

'Is ISO 9000 about quality management, about

being customer driven, or about developing a learning organization? Definitely not,' says James Lynch, corporate quality director at Sun Microsystems and operations chairman for the American Electronics Association TQC steering committee.

Harsher still is Motorola, 1988 winner of the Malcolm Baldrige National Quality Award: 'We're critical of how ISO is being used and misrepresented. Some recently certified companies, through advertisements, imply that a customer can be assured of high standards and reliable products and service as a result of ISO 9000 certification. This is false. ISO 9000 certification has no direct connection to a product or service' – part of a long statement by Richard Buetow, senior vice-president and director of quality at Motorola.

The basic problem faced by management today is that we are entering the twenty-first century with organizations designed to function in the past. We need something entirely different. We need re-engineering.

Still, I would be the first to admit that unless re-engineering is done correctly, it stands a good chance of going the way of the dinosaurs. One of the fears of re-engineering, critics caution, is the 'wholesale dismantling' of systems that, while imperfect, none the less work. Redesigning complex processes from scratch on a clean sheet of paper can be traumatic. Organizations have improved greatly over the years and not by throwing out everything they had, argue those resistant to change.

While care is required in managing the change, too much caution is shortsighted. I have no tolerance for people who say re-engineering is too ambitious. I acknowledge, however, that companies contemplating it must be committed to the project, both emotionally and financially. For example, to be remade completely a company can expect to pay tens of thousands of dollars a month for anything from two to four years.

This book is intended for members of senior management who have the mandate to commit their organizations to a journey of change. It is organized logically and takes the reader on a re-engineering voyage, step by step, with detours to visit related issues such as benchmarking, leadership and creativity. Re-engineering is not an easy task but to facilitate understanding I have organized it in four simple steps. Step One discusses the change imperative. Step Two deals with vision and targets. Step Three concentrates on redesigning, building and implementing, and Step Four is concerned with long-term sustenance of results. Many re-engineering projects fail largely because the accompanying change is not managed well, so this final step is of paramount importance.

Re-engineering has suffered from a bad press lately. This is due mainly to the fact that it is still very much misunderstood. Done well, re-engineering delivers quantum leaps in productivity, and hence profitability. Just as the world is beginning to think that consultants have milked the re-engineering cash cow just about dry and that any concept prefixed with the word 're' is going out of date, the demand for re-engineering continues to grow. I have therefore found it necessary to update this book and the second edition includes five new chapters.

An organization's vision drives its strategy and then its goals and objectives. Often somewhere along the line, there is a disconnection between vision and actionable objectives. The management tool which is taking some parts of the world by storm – the Balanced Scorecard – is introduced and explained in Chapter 3, 'Using the Balanced Scorecard'.

Leadership remains a key to successful implementation of change initiatives and while I touched on leadership in the first edition, I feel I need to reinforce my point. Hence Chapter 8, 'A Fish Rots from the Head'.

In the last couple of years, I have seen with increasing frequency companies putting the proverbial cart before the horse as far as the computerization of processes is concerned. Computerizing obsolete processes is tantamount to cementing cow paths. Technology, if it is to be used, must be used intelligently. I don't claim to be a *technogeek* but feel compelled to share what I know in Chapter 12, 'Information Technology as an Enabler'.

What will happen to re-engineering? Indeed, what will happen to the world as we know it? Prophets of doom continue to predict re-engineering's death as they try to forecast what the next 'flavour of the month' is. At the risk of being labelled a soothsayer, I share my thoughts in Chapter 14, 'What Next?'.

Being based in Asia – and being Asian myself – naturally exposes me more to Asian organizations although I have consulted throughout Europe and the USA. Is re-engineering any different here in Asia? Read about it in Chapter 15, 'The Asian Way'.

Michael Loh

Acknowledgements

*No man is an island. Without the work and
understanding of so many experts and practitioners,
I would never have been able to produce this
manuscript.*

*I hope that this single, overriding recognition of
that fact will express my deep appreciation and
admiration for their work.*

*My thanks go to G.I., Hanjin, Hanlie and
Hanxie for allowing me time off to work on this book
and to Ivy Wong for typing it.*

ML

Part I

STEP ONE

Establishing the Change Imperative

Chapter 1
Positioning for Change

If you want to make a success of your re-engineering effort the one thing you have to do is to establish a change imperative. Do you really want your organization to change? How badly do you want that change? How is the climate in your organization now? What do you want it to be like?

Imagine going to work, walking into your office or factory, and encountering a cheerful, vibrant and stimulating atmosphere. In talking to employees about a forthcoming deadline or project, you hear only enthusiasm and commitment. They are eager to work hard, listen to your ideas, and graciously share their own. Some of the employees brainstorm about possible glitches and how to boost sales and profits. They banter with you and among themselves, their easy humour showing that they enjoy work and that they like and respect you.

As the day progresses, they are on the phone, meeting among themselves, intent at the computer, sometimes coming to you with creative and proactive ideas. Each project is approached with a sense of urgency and professionalism. Some actually finish ahead of schedule. These diligent employees are continuously looking for ways to improve their product or service, to deliver it faster and better, and to upgrade their skills.

When someone volunteers to take charge, others are quick to join in and help. They know that on another project, they themselves may be the leader and need support. They're confident that you value their inputs; you listen to their suggestions and are flexible enough to accommodate each of them. The atmosphere is charged by employee voices that are sincere and enthusiastic, human and personal. No awkward silences when bosses pass by. No anxious scribbling of pass-the-buck memos. No rumour mongering. No gossips. No politicking. No backstabbing. No ungrateful people who take and take and give nothing in return. No busybodies prying into other people's private lives. No immature managers taken in by *agents provocateurs* and manipulators with hidden agendas. No sullen hostility between employees. The atmosphere is adult and mature. The usual me-versus-you antagonism has been replaced by a sharing of responsibilities and a feeling of 'we're all in this together'.

Teamwork and partnerships, rather than the old rigid ladders, make up the company structure. Employees are empowered to make decisions. Checks and controls are reduced.

Perhaps most remarkable about this new atmosphere is a feeling of respect. From the flexible schedules to the fair salaries and benefits to the sharing of vital information, the company shows that it truly cares about people, and employees reciprocate this trust with gratefulness and loyalty.

This is a sketch of a healthy company. This kind of organization may sound far-fetched – a corporate Utopia that only dreamers or the very naïve would believe in. For many companies, it is. But among the millions of businesses, some are quietly, decisively re-engineering themselves into healthy companies. They're driven by an unshakable conviction that only a healthy company will be alive and competitive in the coming years.

In every company there is a culture, a belief system shared by an organization's members. This strong, widely shared core value, sometimes referred to as the collective programming of the mind, is the way people do things. Organizational culture sets the pace and establishes norms at the workplace.

Organizational culture

The following story illustrates norms at work. Eddie deftly soldered his last wires in the interconnection. That was 18 for the morning – pretty good, he thought. He moved on to the next computer and began to string out the cable for the next job.

'Hi, you're the new kid on the block, aren't you?'

The man was standing beside Eddie, soldering iron in hand.

'Yeah. I came over from the Swindon office – been with the company for ten years.'

'I'm Andrew. Been working here in computer assembly for five years.'

The men shook hands. Andrew walked back to Eddie's last job and looked it over. 'Not bad, Eddie, not bad.' He looked back down the assembly floor. 'How many have you done this morning?'

'Eighteen.'

'Hey, are you trying to spoil the market or what?' Andrew laughed. 'Most of us here think 15 interconnections a day is about right.'

'Well, these I'm doing are quite easy.'

Andrew frowned. 'Yeah, but look what happens. You do 20, maybe 25 easy ones, and make those of us stuck with the difficult jobs look bad. You wouldn't want that to happen, would you?'

'Well, no, of course not.'

'That's the spirit!' Andrew smiled. 'You know, Eddie, we have a drinking group in this company. After work we go for a couple of beers. Then we may visit a massage parlour or two. Not everybody is in it – just the interconnection group. Even a few of them don't make it. You know, we like to keep it sort of exclusive.' He paused. 'Like to come this Friday?'

'Well, okay. Sure . . . Andrew, what does Steve think about the number of jobs a day?'

'You mean our foreman Steve? He don't know the difference, and if he did, what difference would it make? You can't find good interconnection men right off the streets. He goes along – him and the rest of management, Patrick, Bernie, Steve, Douglas etc., don't know how fast the work should go, and they don't bother him and so he don't bother us.'

Eddie looked at his next job. He was doing the toughest kind of interconnection, and he knew that any reasonably skilled person should be able to do at least 40 jobs a day on most of the other interconnections. This was going to be a relaxing job. He didn't like skiving, but these people were going to be working with him every day, and he wasn't about to get off on the wrong foot with them. Besides, he liked beer.

'Why don't you come over to the loo with me?' Andrew said. 'We can have a smoke. We've got plenty of time.'

The above exchange is a classic example of how new

members suppress their own standards to conform to existing norms and fit into the group.

Conforming to group norms

A norm is an idea or belief about behaviour expected to be displayed by members of a group. The extent to which group members comply with norms affects the productivity of groups. Lack of conformity to group norms may result in verbal abuse, physical threats, ostracism or ejection from the group. In any organization the deviant's place in the hierarchy is low. The deviant is an individual who deviates from the norms but is still somewhat tolerated by others in the group. It is the isolate who falls at the lowest level of the hierarchy. The isolate does not meet group norms; therefore the group rejects, and does not value, this member.

Norms result from the combination of members' personality characteristics, the situation, the task, the leadership in the organization and the historical traditions of the group. Norms develop through interaction of group members and reinforcement of behaviours by the group. Norms are among the sentiments that develop as group members continue to interact with one another. Very often it is a case of 'monkey see, monkey do'.

The manager of a company has a reputation for shouting at anyone she is in contact with – her subordinates, her clients, her consultants. This woman has never been seen to talk intelligently. She is always emotional, banging tables, screaming her head off. 'Just like her boss,' say critics. When her boss goes to a restaurant, he shouts at waitresses and asks them to read his lips when they cause minor irritations.

In one Asian company run by expatriate Danes, the men at the helm are of the opinion that no Asian can be trusted, Asians are stupid, everything can be negotiated and all arms can be twisted. The result is an immature, neurotic, out-of-touch, paranoid yet arrogant organization full of distrust and disdain for the locals.

Norms exist outside business as well. An entire country may subscribe to a norm that issues should be openly debated in the name of democracy, human rights should be exercised to the extent that even criminals ought to be respected and be permitted to enjoy lucrative rewards from book and movie rights, that public opinion and aggressive lobbying can even alter the behaviour of foreign governments. Some elements from such a country fail to understand that what for them is a norm may not be a norm for others.

Norms also have the power to regulate the behaviour of group members rather than their thoughts or feelings. Members may believe one thing but do another to maintain membership in a group. For example, during the Iran–Contra affair in

1985–7, there were several meetings in which the US president and his aides, such as Lt Col. Oliver North, National Security Advisor Robert McFarlane and CIA Director William Casey, discussed the sale of arms in exchange for American hostages. Secretary of State George Schultz and Secretary of Defense Caspar Weinberger were known to be against the sale of arms to Iran, even indirectly through Israel. The president and others favoured such arms sales and were eager to achieve the release of American hostages held in Iran. Schultz and Weinberger did not attend meetings in which further arms sales were authorized. Although it is not clear whether they were excluded by the members or excluded themselves by not attending, norms clearly affected the meetings and outcomes. From the group's perspective, the norms were to approve the arms transfer. Anyone who continued to argue against the transfer would not be in the group. Schultz and Weinberger knew they were in the minority and were making it uncomfortable for the president. If they wanted to maintain their valued membership in the president's cabinet as heads of two of the most powerful agencies of the executive branch, they knew they should not continue to cause trouble. Thus the group norms regarding how presidential advisers are supposed to act may have led them to decide not to attend.

Pressures to conform to group norms can be

powerful determinants of group performance. Norms affect setting goals, defining behaviours that are appropriate for members, and restricting behaviours of members. Conformity to group norms may result in serious problems, such as unsafe work practices. For example, at a manufacturing plant strict rules were in place regarding the use of gloves in the drill press area. Company safety regulations prohibited the use of gloves for certain tasks because of the safety hazard involved if the gloves, and the worker's hands along with them, became caught in the rapidly spinning drill bit. However, the norms of the group dictated the common practice for drill press operators, which was to use gloves for several steps in the drilling process. On-the-job training, health and safety training classes, and numerous strict warnings were given to the drill press operators, but the group norms were too strong. Finally one morning an operator's gloves did become caught in a spinning drill bit, grabbing two of the worker's fingers, seriously twisting them, and resulting in their amputation. Obviously, this worker and the company paid a very high price for conformity to group norms.

The more the group's members are committed to the group's task, the more the group generates its own rules. Re-engineering often ultimately involves the destruction and changing of group norms, encouraging people to increase their productivity by

Changing group norms

doing things differently. Therefore, understanding the concept of norms must precede any action on them.

Once a progressive norm pervades an organization, great and wonderful things can happen. For example, who can imagine a group of taxi drivers achieving a stock exchange listing? That's what happened in Singapore in June 1994.

The story started much earlier, in 1970, at a time when unregulated (and uncomfortable) taxis had the run of the roads. Inspired by the National Trade Union Congress, a co-operative named Comfort was formed. With an initial membership of 1 000 taxis and 200 minibus operators, the co-operative set out to provide a reliable and efficient public transport service. Twenty years on, with some 10 000 taxis, and more than 500 000 passengers daily, Comfort has become the largest taxi operator not just in Singapore but in the world. The Comfort group today comprises four companies. In the last financial year, the group achieved an excess of income over expenditure before taxation and appropriation of S$25.77 million. It was listed on the main board of the Singapore Stock Exchange. As a result of the listing, about 5 500 of its taxi drivers are in line for a multi-million dollar windfall.

If they choose to sell the shares they own, they stand to realize capital gains of S$9 500 to S$24 500, based on a S$1 strike price and their original S$500 investment. (In 1970, these drivers had paid S$500 each for their initial stake to become members of the co-operative.)

The other companies in the group are also in transport-related business. When I spoke to Dr Wan Soon Bee, the chairman of the group, and Sam Chong Keen, its managing director, at that time, and their senior management colleagues about re-engineering – the management imperative of the 1990s – I was impressed with their foresight and progressive spirit. From a co-operative the group is now a commercial giant. The transition involved a change not only in behaviour but in attitude or mindset. It is fashionable these days to talk about paradigm shift and this is precisely what the co-operative went through.

Contrast Comfort with the story of the railroad tycoons in the USA. Even if you didn't have an MBA, sooner or later you'd discover the lessons of the railroad tycoons. They thought they had reached the top, what with their rails criss-crossing the country. That was why they did not pay much attention to all the new roads and to all the trucks that were starting to roll on them. They ignored the potential of shipping. In those days if you asked a railway millionaire he would say 'I'm in the railroad business'. So the tycoons stayed in their 'comfort zones'. They were in the railroad business, after all. Well, the lessons of history tell us that it was such thinking that finished them off.

The leaders at Comfort didn't think they were in just the taxi business, they reckoned they were in the transport business. They established a workshop with 200 repair bays. It became one of the largest and most sophisticated vehicle repair workshops in Singapore. They established a vehicle inspection centre equipped with state-of-the-art technology. They provided consultancy to the Asian Development Bank on its road overlay improvement project in Bangladesh. Yes, they have gone international – operations were started in China, and investment opportunities in Vietnam and Myanmar are being explored.

Change is a difficult process but, apart from death and income taxes, it is about the only thing which is constant. An entity which is not changing and evolving may take on all semblance of life, but in reality it has already died. It has stopped growing. And it has stopped learning.

Creating a learning organization
The concept of the learning organization became popular in the early 1990s. Management thinkers are still not in agreement as to what exactly is a learning organization but it has been described as a place where people continually expand their capacity to create results, where new and expansive patterns of thinking are nurtured, where collective aspiration is set free and

where people are continually learning how to learn together. Organizations are seen as learning by encoding inferences from history into routines that guide behaviour.

Recently the board at Bank Dharmala, one of the largest banks in Indonesia, was confronted with a difficult decision – to hire a brand new president director who would embark on a massive re-engineering effort and risk losing seven experienced, long-serving general managers who felt threatened, or to keep the seven loyal managers and forget about organizational renewal. The board ultimately decided to hire the new man. Taking umbrage, the seven general managers quit. Titra Adysurya Sutanto, the president director, transformed the bank into a learning organization. The next time the books closed, the bank's profitability had increased a hundredfold, not 100 per cent but a hundred times more.

In fiscal year 1993 Citicorp paid its chairman, John Reed, US$6.2 million in cash and stock, triple his pay in 1992. The reason for Citicorp's generosity was the outstanding job Reed did in nursing the company back to health after it had plunged dangerously near the bankruptcy level. Citicorp also granted Reed options on 450 000 shares of its stock. These options may be worth US$21 million in ten years if the stock appreciates at a rate of 10 per cent a year, less, but not by much, if the stock's market value increases more slowly.

What the compensation consultant of Citicorp seems to have lost sight of in awarding Reed such princely sums for his 'vision and tenacity in overseeing Citicorp's return to corporate strength' is that it was Reed himself who had been responsible for the company's decline and near fall. It was the same John Reed who, in 1992, had so mismanaged Citicorp that its cash dividend had been first reduced, then omitted altogether. For his outstanding leadership and competency, John Reed had been paid US$2.07 million in salary in 1992, surely one of the most generous compensation packages in American business history considering the disastrous results achieved. It is highly doubtful whether any of Reed's subordinates would have been so generously rewarded for undoing their own earlier mistakes. Sometimes one wonders if organizations ever learn from the lessons of the past.

A learning organization should not just be an organization skilled at creating, acquiring and transferring knowledge, it should also be an organization that modifies its behaviour to reflect new knowledge and insights.

This definition begins with a simple truth that new

ideas are vital if change is to take place. New ideas are sometimes created *de novo*, through flashes of insight or creativity; at other times they arrive from outside the organization or are communicated by knowledgeable insiders. Whatever the source, these ideas are the trigger for organizational improvement. But they cannot by themselves create a learning organization. Without accompanying changes in the way that work is done, only the potential for improvement exists.

This is a stringent test as it rules out a number of obvious candidates for learning organizations. Most universities fail to qualify, as do many consulting firms. Even General Motors, despite its efforts to improve performance, is found wanting. General Motors has had little success in revamping its manufacturing practices, even though its managers are experts on lean manufacturing, JIT production, and the requirements for improved quality of work life. All these organizations have been effective at creating or acquiring new knowledge but notably less successful in applying that knowledge to their own activities. Total Quality Management, for example, is now taught at many business schools, yet the number using it to guide their own decision making is very small. Consultants advise clients on strategy and organizational effectiveness, but are notorious for their own political infighting and factionalism and for what *Fortune* refers to as 'clunky' methodologies.

Are we using what we have learned

Organizations that do pass the definitional test have, by contrast, become adept at translating new knowledge into new ways of behaving.

Learning organizations are not built overnight. Senior management must foster an environment that is conducive to learning. Boundaries must be opened up and the exchange of ideas stimulated. General Electric's CEO, Jack Welch, considers this to be such a powerful stimulant of change that he has made 'boundarylessness' a cornerstone of the company's strategy for the 1990s.

Organizational life cycle

If an organization continues to learn and the group norms are healthy, that organization will stay in its prime for a long time.

Like products, corporations also go through a life cycle: conception, infancy, go-go, adolescence, prime, steady, aristocracy, bureaucracy and death.

At conception stage, the organization is not yet born. It exists only as an idea. An infant organization is a new organization. The go-go stage is a period of all-out growth, leading to adolescence when an organization arrives at a crossroad and has to decide what core businesses it should concentrate on. Once that decision is made, the organization stays prime. This is the optimum point of the life cycle where the organization has come of age and achieves a balance between self-control and flexibility. Beyond prime is steady and this is usually the start of decline – the organization begins to lose its flexibility and suffers from an attitude that says, 'If it ain't broke, don't fix it'. The organization mellows and then reaches aristocracy – a process of increasing self-preservation and distancing from clients. Next comes bureaucracy – not Weber's ideal bureaucracy but bureaucracy as we know it today – top-heavy organizations with antiquated internal processes whose people are mostly empowered only to say no. Internal politicking is the order of the day and external customers are considered a nuisance. It is on a life-support system, justifying its existence not by the fact that it is functioning well, but by the fact that it exists. Such an organization may linger for a long time, surviving a protracted coma. The actual death may take years! Death is prolonged only because the organization's commitment is not to its clients, but to political interests that keep it from dying. If the organization depended on clients, it would have died already, because its clients would have deserted a long time ago.

As competition becomes fiercer and operating costs continue to rise, organizations can no longer work with outdated ideas and gargantuan processes. It is more critical for organizations to change. Once you have decided that you have no choice but to change, you then need to create vision and targets.

Are we really here (legacy) commitment

19

Part II
STEP TWO

Creating Vision and Targets

Chapter 2
Envisioning the Future

You cannot just start re-engineering, just as you cannot travel to a destination without first putting together a plan or an itinerary.

Planning is more than verbalizing or articulating organizational objectives. Remember the five Ps – poor planning makes for piss-poor performance. An unsound plan will end up being a wish list. Nothing more.

The path for organizational renewal and change must start with a structured process. Once in place, such a plan can prove invaluable. It can help crystallize and formalize the vision you have of your organization and enable you to capitalize on internal strengths and external opportunities.

McDonald's was once a hamburger stand. Then it was a fast food hamburger place. If you compare the McDonald's of the 1970s to the McDonald's of the 1990s, you'll see a dramatically different, reinvented business. How much of its total sales then came from breakfast? From the drive-in windows? From lunch orders on the fax machine?

There's an old joke about three types of people: those who make things happen, those who wait for things to happen, and those who wonder what the hell happened? This book is a clarion call to you to join that first group.

Andy Grove, the CEO of Intel, once said that 'a corporation is a living organism and it has to continually shed its skin. Methods have to change. Focus has to change. Values have to change. The sum total of those changes is transformation.' Re-engineering can make that transformation a reality.

You start by first attaining consensus on your corporate vision. Collectively, you and members of your senior management must decide what all of you want your organization to be. A vision is a visualization, a dream, a clear mental picture of a future desired state which your organization hopes to attain. A vision is the difference between short-term 'hits' and long-term change. A vision should stretch the expectations and challenge the *status quo*. And of course it should eventually translate into actions, behaviours and outcomes.

Ford Motor Company's vision for its accounts payable department that it should be streamlined, together with re-engineering, resulted in its North American accounts payable department staffing being reduced from 500 to 125!

All successful individuals and organizations have one thing in common: the power and depth of their vision of the future. A positive vision of the future is essential for providing meaning and direction to the present. Having a positive vision of the future is perhaps the most powerful motivator for change you and I possess. It is necessary that we think about, dream about, and ultimately enVISION our own futures. Through the strength of our visions, we empower ourselves to shape the future.

The *sine qua non* of effective change leadership is a shared vision which fosters understanding of, and commitment to, the ultimate goal. Clear actionable visions must be painted to present pictures of what the organization's operating environment will be within a realistic time frame, say, five years from now.

If you haven't carried out a team visioning exercise, start now! An idiot's guide to crafting a vision statement is provided in Figure 2.1. If all you care for are nice sounding statements, then all you need is this tongue-in-cheek approach. First conduct an environmental analysis. This is a diagnosis of the external environment; stakeholders' expectations, government policies, competitors' strategies and actions, and customers' perceptions and needs can all affect profitability and competitiveness. Information is crucial to accurate appraisal, and conducting market research will help you obtain the data you need.

Next do a SWOT (Strength, Weakness, Opportunity, Threat) analysis, by which you can arrive at certain

Team visioning exercise

OUR VISION

1 Select from one to three items from each group below
2 Add your logo
3 Marinate overnight in Scotch and red wine
4 Serve with a straight face

To be a	Company that provides	To	In the rapidly changing
premier	innovative	serve the global marketplace	information-solutions
leading	cost-effective	create shareholder value	business-solutions
pre-eminent	focused	fulfil our covenants with	consumer-solutions
world-class	diversified	our stakeholders	financial-solutions
growing	high-quality	delight our customers	industries
	products		
	services		
	products and services		

Figure 2.1 How not to develop a vision

conclusions about how strengths can be harnessed, and how core competences can be further enhanced.

A core competence is the accumulation of your organization's knowledge and expertise. Such competence is difficult for competitors to copy and is the basis for your competitiveness in the marketplace. It can enable you to gain access to a wide range of markets.

Example of SWOT analysis

Pet Computers, makers of SHERRY computers, under the leadership of its managing director, Ng Gak Seng, conducted a SWOT analysis in 1988. Based on the findings of the analysis, certain measures were taken. As a result sales hit S$20 million the following year and SHERRY computers became the number-one-selling IBM compatible in Singapore. These were Pet Computers' SWOT findings.

Strengths

1   Company has built its good name and image, being the number two in the local market share after IBM.

2   Product is priced at a premium (about the same as ACER, NEC, EPSON, WYSE, MITAC) and yet remains competitive, with sales growing above industry average.

3   Company has progressed very fast over the year –

from shop and office to its present size with 70 employees, sales of S$15 million, and paid capital doubled in a year.

4 Company has established selected overseas markets through its frequent participation in trade fairs. Sales are expected to double in the mid-1990s.

5 Sales staff are frequently being trained by outside consultants. On financial aspects, Coopers & Lybrand has been engaged in study of upgrading plan. Company has regularly been using advertising and promotion consultants, financial consultants etc. to improve its effectiveness.

6 Company has the flexibility to adapt to change: has phased out PC XT (8088) and redundant CGA cards; introduced a slimline range, PRO 386, ETHERNET cards etc.; third party maintenance.

7 With existing marketing networks and image, should be able to tie up with many R & D companies in Japan and USA and be able to market OEM or related products if fund permits.

Weaknesses

1 Company has insufficient funds to grow. Many opportunities have to be forgone or delayed because amount of shareholders' fund is limited.

2 Company has to slow down growth in order to conduct the business within certain margin of safety. Has increased selling price by 5 per cent during the year and has tightened up credit terms to customers in order not to overstretch the business.

3   Company has adopted factoring services, an expensive way of borrowing for its short-term financing. Situation is expected to improve as several bankers have made offers to the company.

4   Company gathers information on an *ad hoc* basis and does not make full use of a consistent, organized information-gathering mechanism, which would improve business decisions, control, cost savings etc. so as to gain an edge over its competitors.

5   Weak bargaining power from the suppliers compared to multinationals. Unable to take advantage of bulk purchases due to tight cash flow.

Opportunities

1   The growing demand for computers and related products will continue in the future – company has yet to explore the many potentials in this industry.

2   Existing marketing networks and image enable the company to market many products with reasonable volume and also obtain many OEM products under company's brand.

3   Has yet to source raw materials and other products from more avenues such as Japan, USA etc. – should further reduce costs. Increased volume would also improve bargaining power of company.

4   Introduction of budgetary control system will result in better control of business and improve effectiveness of the operations – should give rise to

substantial cost savings in the coming years.

5   Many opportunities for the company to have associated business with famous R & D organizations in Japan, USA and Europe. Locally, there are many software houses, computer schools, companies with related computer products who wish to link up with PET.

6   Government is giving support to help many local companies grow and become multinationals.

7   Company has no difficulty in obtaining better facilities and terms from various banks if paid-up capital is increased; with bigger capital base and more outside funds from banks, further opportunities could be realized.

Threats

1   IBM has always been a threat to all makers of IBM compatibles. IBM's price is becoming more competitive and is a threat and fear to its competitors because of its new technology and worldwide recognition for its originality.

2   Rate of technology in this industry is changing and growing rapidly.

Examples of vision statements

A visioning exercise is important. This is to also avoid people talking like John Rock, general manager of General Motor's Oldsmobile Division, who once referred to visioning as 'A bunch of guys take off their ties and coats, go into a motel room for three days, and

put a bunch of "f******" words on a piece of paper –
and then go back to business as usual.'

Before the visioning session, make available samples
of some good vision statements from various organizations to inspire team members and to serve as
examples (see Figures 2.2–2.5).

There has been considerable debate on the
difference between a vision statement and a mission
statement. To avoid that debate, I simply refer to the
whole exercise as 'visioning'. Those who want to split
hairs say that vision statements are goal-like statements,
whereas mission statements are more explicit and are
SMART (Specific, Measurable, Attainable, Realistic
and Trackable).

American International Assurance's mission
statement says 'AIA is committed to being the market
leader in life insurance'.

British Airways wants 'to be the best and most
successful airline in the world, earning good profits in
whatever it does'.

The Wuthelam Group, Singapore, believes in
'nurturing the powerful entrepreneurship spirit
instilled by [our] founder, in seeking out new markets
and unsatisfied customer needs, and in innovative
solutions to satisfy them'.

Marriott, an American hotel chain, takes its corporate vision statement seriously. It helps shape the future success as a global organization by pledging to:
1   Focus on each of its customers, earning their trust and loyalty.
2   Follow the ideals of the Marriott philosophy, most importantly the belief that taking care of its associates is the key to success. Marriott:
    ◆   treats people fairly, ethically, honestly and in a caring manner
    ◆   offers each associate maximum opportunity to grow professionally while maintaining a balance between work and personal needs
    ◆   helps promote women and minorities into all levels of management
    ◆   creates a positive environment that generates teamwork and instils pride.
3   Use Total Quality Management to pioneer new levels of customer satisfaction and value, becoming a model for organizations around the world. Marriott:
    ◆   encourages initiative, openness and innovation
    ◆   supports those who uncover problems and generate solutions.
4   Build profitable, long-term relationships with Marriott's extended family of distributors, franchisees, lenders, owners, shareholders, suppliers, and the communities in which it works.

Figure 2.2   Marriott's vision

AIA (American International Assurance) is Southeast Asia's premier life-insurance company, and is committed to being the market leader in life insurance and to provide:
◆   total life insurance with distinctive one-stop servicing
◆   innovative product design, packaging and development
◆   professional agency force and staff services.
AIA will assist and augment our agency productivity by developing new distribution channels.
AIA will strive to achieve profit and growth commensurate with the objectives of AIG.

Figure 2.3   AIA's mission statement

Wuthelam is a Singapore-based business conglomerate. One thing characterizes companies in the Wuthelam Group – their shared core values and objectives, which are:

VALUES
The Group believes in:

Entrepreneurship
◆ Nurturing the powerful entrepreneurship spirit instilled by its founder in seeking out new markets and unsatisfied customer needs and in innovative solutions to satisfy them.

Partnerships
◆ Cultivating and strengthening productive relationships with our business partners, joint-venture partners, customers, suppliers, employees and governments so the Group can more effectively achieve customer satisfaction.

Fairness
◆ Ensuring that we are fair, and seen to be fair in all our business dealings with partners, customers and suppliers.

OBJECTIVES
The Group seeks to build upon its values to achieve these business objectives:

Profit
◆ To generate profits to ensure a fair return to our shareholders and to fuel the growth that will provide our people with expanded career opportunities.

Customer satisfaction
◆ To provide the best value to our customers by combining the highest quality products and services with competitive prices.

Growth
◆ To pursue steady and sustainable growth through the identification and satisfaction of customers' current and emerging needs.

People
◆ To help our people to develop to their fullest potential, and to gain a sense of satisfaction and pride from their work. To help them to attain an increasing standard of living as the Group grows.

Citizenship
◆ To contribute to the economic and social well-being of every community in which we operate.

Figure 2.4 *Wuthelam's core values and objectives*

Cathay Pacific is a well-known Asian airline with
headquarters in Hong Kong, and they pledge that:
We will continue to be one of the world's most successful
airlines.
We will provide rewarding and enjoyable careers for our
staff who as a team have spontaneous commitment to:
- the highest standards of operational safety and
  efficiency
- outstanding service in the air and on the ground
- constant improvement and innovation to our product
- sustained investment in new technology
- a flexible and speedy response to the market and Hong
  Kong.
This commitment will ensure that our customers 'Arrive In
Better Shape' and provide growing rewards for our
shareholders and staff.
The latest statement of the Cathay Pacific Commitment
reads:
Cathay Pacific Commitment for the 90's
- We will be the best airline of the decade.
- We put safety and security first.
- We will be totally customer-driven.
- We will produce superior financial returns.
- We will provide rewarding and enjoyable careers for our
  staff.
- We accept our responsibility towards the environment.
- We are committed to the communities we serve and to
  the future of Hong Kong.

Figure 2.5   *Cathay Pacific's public statement of commitment*

Cathay Pacific says 'we will be the best airline of the
decade'.

Grace Cocoa's mission statement says 'we are
committed to being the best industrial cocoa and
chocolate company in the world by producing
products and services that meet and anticipate our
customers' needs'.

Here's how you conduct a visionary exercise. Go away for a couple of days. In 1992, Alan J. Wilson, then group manager of the local office of Guardian Royal Exchange, a respected British insurance company, took his management team to Sentosa island off Singapore and held a visioning weekend. Andrew Tan, senior vice-president and general manager of American International Assurance, held a visioning workshop with his managers at Damai Beach, Kuching, Sarawak.

Visioning session

Break up your participants into small groups and appoint someone to serve as a scribe or a facilitator. Ask each group to brainstorm and draft a vision statement. This is a written statement of purpose, crafted to inspire employees to commit to the company's vision. Group members should be asking four questions which capture your organization's reasons for being.

◆ Who are we?

◆ What do we do?

◆ For whom do we do it?

◆ Why do we do it?

Learn from the past

Participants may want to review their organization's past, or at least keep it at the back of their minds. This is sometimes referred to as the Santayana Review, a reference to the philosopher George Santayana, who coined the phrase 'Those who cannot remember the past are condemned to repeat it'. Unfortunately many managers today are indifferent to the past.

A study of more than 150 new products concluded that 'knowledge gained from failures [is] often instrumental in achieving subsequent successes. In the simplest terms, failure is the ultimate teacher'. IBM's 360 computer series, for example, one of the most popular and profitable ever built, was based on the technology of the failed Stretch computer that preceded it. Some organizations have established processes that require their managers to think periodically about the past and learn from their mistakes.

Boeing did so immediately after its difficulties with the 737 and 747 plane programmes. Both planes were introduced with much fanfare and also with serious problems. To ensure that the problems were not repeated, senior managers commissioned a high-level employee group, Project Homework, to compare the development processes of the 737 and 747 with those of the 707 and 727, two of the company's most profitable planes. The group was asked to develop a set of 'lessons learned' that could be applied to future projects. After working for three years, it produced hundreds of recommendations and an inch-thick booklet. Several members of the team were then transferred to the 757 and 767 start-ups and, guided by experience, they produced the most successful, error-free launches in Boeing's history.

Xerox studied its product development process, examining three troubled products in an effort to understand why the company's new business initiatives failed so often.

At the heart of this approach is a mindset that enables organizations to recognize the value of productive failure as contrasted with unproductive success. A productive failure is one that leads to insight and understanding and thus an addition to the commonly held wisdom of the organization. An unproductive success occurs when something goes well, but nobody knows how or why. IBM's founder, Thomas Watson, Sr, apparently understood the distinction well. Company lore has it that a younger manager, after losing $10 million in a risky venture, was called into Watson's office. The frightened young man began by saying: 'I guess you want my resignation'. Watson replied, 'You can't be serious. We just spent $10 million educating you.'

Presentation of the statement

At the end of the brainstorming, group members should craft the vision statement to make it clear, concise and actionable. Modify, modify and modify until you are satisfied and ready to present it when all the groups reconvene. You are embarking on the first critical step in making vision a reality for every member of the company.

As one group, review and edit all statements presented to arrive at one final statement which best captures what you want to say and which is acceptable to all.

Senior executives from the Singapore branch of the Guardian Royal Exchange worked on a vision statement which reads as follows: 'GRE is committed to being one of Singapore's most successful insurance companies and to being an industry leader in providing quality service, consistently.'

The other components of your vision statement should include:

The glossary   which defines key words and phrases in the statement, thus preventing differing interpretations of the vision. This is GRE's example:

> *GRE – each and everyone of us at GRE, working together as a team, united in our vision, and supporting one another, to achieve the best results.*

COMMITTED – loyalty to the company's vision.

MOST SUCCESSFUL INSURANCE COMPANIES – consistently achieving profitable growth and maintaining a positive reputation and position in the community.

INDUSTRY LEADER – GRE is recognized as a leader in the setting of service standards.

QUALITY SERVICE – striving to provide innovative and value-added service to meet customers' expectations.

CONSISTENTLY – we believe in continuous improvement for the benefit of internal and external customers.

The guiding principles the crucial values that guide employees' relationships with clients and one another. Here is GRE's example:

1   *We strive to constantly improve the quality of our service.*

2   *We are customer-driven and we strive to out-perform our competitors in meeting our customers' needs and expectations.*

3   *We provide competent, timely and problem-free service.*

4   *We communicate effectively.*

5   *We are open and approachable to our business partners and to each other.*

6   *We are a sound and reliable long-term business partner.*

7   *We maintain a high level of ethics and integrity in everything we do.*

8   *We work effectively as a team:*

◆   *recognizing each other's strengths and weaknesses and complementing one another*

◆   *respecting the values and contributions of each individual*

◆   *relying on the participation and initiative of each individual*

◆   *making clear decisions.*

9   *We take pride in the work we do and we have a sense of ownership in our work.*

Follow-up

Identify areas for change at each level of the organizational hierarchy and communicate to staff at each level that they are expected to assist in re-engineering in order that the vision will become a reality. This cascading or roll-down consensus process will form the foundation of your re-engineering process. Too many off-site training, boot camps or 'powwow' sessions have ended up with no tangible results. This is because of no post-event follow-up. Management is being neglectful of its duty if it enthuses people to a high level of motivation but provides no tools for them to channel their motivation into action.

S.   Nithianandan,   head   of   manpower   and

organization development at Malayan Banking, organized a 'road show' and visited every Malayan Banking branch throughout Malaysia for the roll-down. This reduced resistance considerably and paved the way for permanent change.

Chapter 3
Using the Balanced Scorecard

Now that you've got your vision the trick is to make it work.

Too often in organizations there is no connection between the vision and the implementation of that vision. The disconnection is caused by obstacles that are the result of the traditional way in which organizations are managed. The traditional management style is usually based on financial considerations and the top-down, command and control model of management.

The most obvious obstacle is that most organizations end up with a vision which is not viable. If the vision and mission statements cannot be translated into actions, the consequence is fragmentation and suboptimization of efforts. Lacking clarity and consensus, different groups within the organization pursue different agendas and the result is chaos.

Must be able to translate into action

The story goes that when President John F. Kennedy visited Cape Canaveral at the start of the 1960s, he came across a man in overalls, and the president asked him what his job was. 'My job,' replied the cleaner quickly, 'is to help put a man on the moon by the end of the decade.'

Despite the best intentions of those at the top,

[handwritten annotations in margins:]
Goals — objectives that make sense & have meaning & are 'real' level

Must be able to translate the vision into workable actions at local levels

So what does that mean to 'me'

The Key — continuity

statements about becoming 'best in class', 'the number one supplier' or an 'empowered organization' don't translate easily into operational terms that provide useful guides to action at the local level.

It is not enough to have a clear vision when there is no mechanism to share that vision across the organization and make it work. For people to act on the words in vision and strategy statements, those statements must be expressed as an integrated set of objectives and measures, agreed upon by all senior executives, that describe the long-term drivers of success.

The cascading or roll-down consensus process mentioned in the last chapter is therefore of paramount importance. At each level of the organization employees must know what is expected of them in specific, measurable terms.

This is where the second obstacle occurs. Specific measures should concentrate not just on the attainment of financial goals but also on equally significant non-financial aspects of an organization. Robert Kaplan and David Norton, the recognized architects of the Balanced Scorecard management/ measurement system (see Figure 3.1), advocate that organizations use four measures – finance, customer knowledge, internal business processes, and learning and growth – to align individual, organizational and

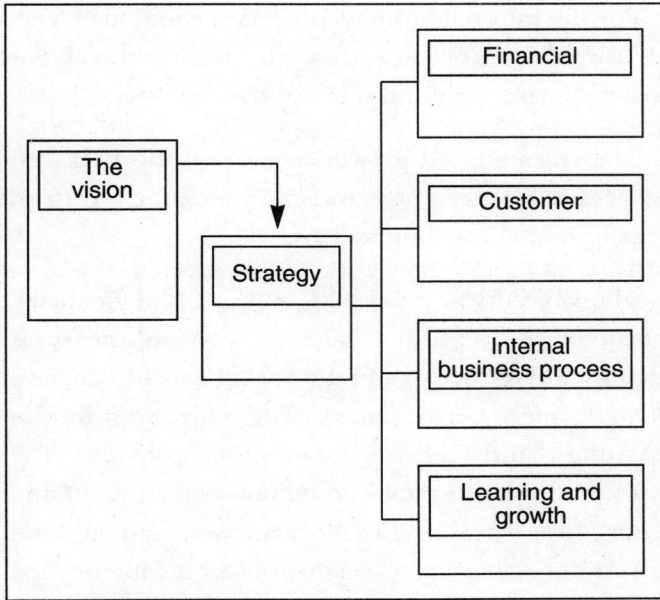

Figure 3.1 *The Balanced Scorecard*

cross-departmental initiatives. The Balanced Scorecard enables management to see the breadth and totality of company operations.

For the customer section of the Balanced Scorecard, companies identify the customer and market segments in which they have chosen to compete. This enables companies to align their core customer outcome measures – satisfaction, loyalty, retention, acquisition and profitability – to targeted customers and market segments.

Common Sales Incen - Shared Rewards
Dane

???

Does this mean People Communicate Management Style

For the internal business process section, managers identify the processes that are most critical for achieving customer and shareholder objectives.

The learning and growth section on the Balanced Scorecard develops objectives and measures to drive organizational learning and growth.

The objectives established by using the financial, customer and internal business process measures identify where the organization must excel to achieve breakthrough performance. The objectives in the learning and growth measure provide the infrastructure to enable ambitious objectives in the other three measures to be achieved, and are the drivers for achieving excellent outcomes in the first three scorecard measures.

You can see that the Balanced Scorecard is so named because it is a tool organized around four distinct perspectives – financial, customer, internal, and innovation and learning. The name reflected the balance between short- and long-term objectives, between financial and non-financial measures, between lagging and leading indicators, and between external and internal performance perspectives.

Pay/choice

Measurement is important. People behave according to how their performance is measured. Consequently a key element of any re-engineering effort is the establishment of new and meaningful performance metrics. Many companies, unfortunately, neglect this critical task. They may ignore the issue entirely (leaving old performance standards in place), or they may fail to measure progress toward new goals. In either case, the company will see lessened benefit from its re-engineering effort. If outmoded performance metrics are permitted to linger, the organization will perform according to outmoded objectives.

Kaplan and Norton first wrote about the scorecard concept in an article, 'The Balanced Scorecard – measures that drive performance', in the *Harvard Business Review* (1992). A second article, 'Putting the Balanced Scorecard to work', was published in the *Harvard Business Review* (1993). A third article, also published in the *Harvard Business Review*, was entitled 'Using the Balanced Scorecard as a strategic management system' (1996).

They then wrote a book, *Translating Strategy into Action: the Balanced Scorecard*, which was published in 1996. Their argument is that financial measures alone are inadequate for guiding and evaluating the journey that information age companies must make to create future value through investment in customers, suppliers, employees, process, technology and innovation.

Communicate —

creating milestone

A third obstacle is the inadequacies of the feedback mechanism. Most management systems today provide feedback only about short-term, operational perform-ance, with the bulk of this feedback on financial measures. More often than not, little or no feedback is given on the implementation of the strategy. In one organization I'm acquainted with, the annual strategy exercise is like this: the managing director submits his plans for the year to head office; head office responds with suggestions on how the plans should be modified; the plans are modified in the places where the managing director felt that modifications could be tolerated (the rest simply ignored) and sent to head office once again. At this stage, head office will respond yet another time exhorting the managing director to please comply with the suggested modifications. More exchanges inevitably follow and by the time the noise quietens down it is August and the plans are filed in the filing cabinet, never to be looked at again.

Summary

The vision drives the formulation of the strategy. The strategy should encompass financial and non-financial objectives. Feedback on performance should be made available. And if you are looking for more than just a tactical or an operational measurement system, consider using the Balanced Scorecard. Innovative companies are using the scorecard as a strategic management system, to manage their strategy over the long term. They are using the measurement aspect of the scorecard to accomplish critical management processes, that is, to:

◆ clarify and translate vision and strategy

◆ communicate and link strategic objectives and measures

◆ plan, set targets, and align strategic initiatives

◆ enhance strategic feedback and learning.

However, the real power of the Balanced Scorecard becomes evident when it is transformed from a measurement system to a management system. As more and more companies work with the Balanced Scorecard, they see how it can be used to:

◆ clarify and gain consensus about strategy

◆ communicate strategy throughout the organization

◆ align departmental and personal goals to the strategy

◆ link strategic objectives to long-term targets and annual budgets

◆ identify and align strategic initiatives

◆ perform periodic and systematic strategic reviews

◆ obtain feedback to learn about and improve strategy.

Chapter 4
Benchmarking Your Way to the Top!

Now that you have vision to strive for, you will want to set standards. This can be done through benchmarking. This chapter is a detour to discuss this important subject.

What can mail order giant LL Bean teach Xerox to help them compete more successfully against Japanese copier manufacturers? How can Bath Iron Works learn the secrets of preventive maintenance by studying procedures at Walt Disney World? How can companies from different industries learn from each other? They can – through benchmarking, i.e. studying the successes of those companies and adapting them to their own business applications. Almost anything can be benchmarked. Xerox, the concept's creator, has applied it to billing, warehousing and automated manufacturing. The premise is basic: benchmark outstanding companies whose business processes are analogous to your own. Benchmarking identifies those practices that have resulted in outstanding performance of successful companies. It identifies practices that can be adapted to the benchmarking companies' business applications. The greatest benefit comes from studying *practices* – the way that work is done – rather than results, and from involving line managers in the process. Thus benchmarking is an operational process of continuous learning and adaptation that results in the development of an improved organization. Like re-engineering, such continuous improvement is not limited to incremental gains; it also implies a need for rapid breakthroughs. More importantly, benchmarking establishes standards of performance.

Roger Milliken, CEO of Milliken Company, in his address at the US National Quality Forum, following his company's acceptance of the Malcolm Baldridge National Quality Award, referred to benchmarking as SIS – Stealing Ideas Shamelessly. Motorola even used the code name 'Bandit' to identify its pocket pager project, which was built by incorporating the best practices of many companies. Since the term 're-engineering' was first used in the book by Hammer and Champy, published in 1993, it has been copied and used for a variety of applications. However, benchmarking is not just copying from other companies. As W. Edwards Deming has stated: 'It is a hazard to copy. It is necessary to understand the theory of what one wishes to do.' Benchmarking is more than just copying.

Westinghouse regards benchmarking as an integrated tool within its Total Quality Improvement Process for 'identifying best practices, wherever they exist, implementing and communicating those practices throughout Westinghouse to improve competitive performance and preserve our core competencies.' The Westinghouse productivity and quality centre's course on benchmarking uses the following definition:

> *Benchmarking is a continuous search for and application of significantly better practices that leads to superior competitive performance.*

As early as the late 1800s, Frederick Taylor's work on the application of the scientific method of business had encouraged comparison of work processes. During the Second World War it became a common business practice for companies to 'check' with other companies to determine standards for pay, work loads, safety, and other business hygiene factors. Taiichi Ohno, former vice-president of manufacturing for Toyota, described the Japanese post-Second World War efforts at benchmarking:

> *Following World War II, American products flowed into Japan – chewing gum and Coca-Cola, even the jeep. The first US-style supermarket appeared in the mid-1950s. And as more and more Japanese people visited the United States, they saw the intimate relationship between the supermarket and the style of daily life in America. Consequently, this type of store became the rage in Japan.*

Ohno further applied his observations of the supermarket by using shelf restocking as an analogy for his development of the JIT (Just-In-Time) inventory management method. 'From the supermarket we got the idea of viewing the earlier process in a production line as a kind of store.' The supermarket analogy provided Ohno with an example of an enabling process from which he developed the *kanban* system for inventory flow management.

Many observers have described Japanese business people as 'copycats' who have excelled only in the art of imitation. This is not true – the Japanese have been applying the practice of benchmarking to their product and process developments as a means to cut the time it takes to implement improvements and bring products to the market. Paul Howell, writing in the *Houston Chronicle* (December 1991), made the following observation:

> *The Japanese excel at benchmarking, at exhaustively analyzing the best companies in each industry, then continually improving on their performance until the Japanese products and services then become the best.*

The four-step approach

Benchmarking uses a basic four-step approach. The four steps follow the fundamental quality method as described by Deming: plan, do, check, act.

In the first step, planning the benchmarking study, you select and define the process that is to be studied; identify the measures of process performance;

evaluate your organization's own capability at this process; and determine which companies should be studied.

The second step in benchmarking is to conduct secondary and primary research. This includes an investigation of public disclosures about the particular process at target companies. It is important to learn as much as possible before making any direct contact because, strange as it may seem, many companies are completely unaware of what has been written about them in the press and trade publications. (The press-clipping service of any credible public relations firm can easily handle that.) More benefits can be derived if direct communication with companies includes site visits to make detailed observations.

The third step in benchmarking is analysis of the gathered data to determine study findings and recommendations. The analysis comprises several aspects: determining the magnitude of the performance gaps between companies, using the benchmarking metrics identified during the planning step; and identifying the process enablers that facilitated the performance improvements at the successful companies.

Listening to customers is important. David Cave, region manager (Singapore, Malaysia, Indonesia, Philippines) of Dow Corning, engaged consultants to interview the company's clients before embarking on the establishment of service standards.

At Singapore's Kandang Kerbau hospital, the world's largest maternity hospital, management conducted focus group meetings with patients to obtain feedback on how the hospital can improve its services.

At Motorola, members of the operating and policy committee, including the CEO, meet personally and on a regular basis with customers. At Worthington Steel, all machine operators make periodic trips to customers' factories to discuss their needs.

Sometimes customers can't articulate their needs or remember even the most recent problems they have had with a product or service. If that is the case, organizations must make observations at the customers' premises. Xerox goes to the extent of employing a number of anthropologists at its Palo Alto research centre to observe users of new document products in their offices. Digital Equipment has developed an interactive process called 'contextual inquiry' that is used by software engineers to observe users of new technologies as they go about their work. Milliken has created 'first-delivery teams' that accompany the first shipment of all products; team members follow the product through the customer's production process to see how it is used and then develop ideas for further improvement. Cognitive scientists have observed that it is very difficult to become knowledgeable in a passive way. Actively experiencing something is considerably more valuable than having it described.

Benchmarking, however, is more than just partying with customers or 'industrial tourism' – *ad hoc* 'feel good' or relationship-building visits made by an organization's top guns to successful organizations. What's more, it can be expensive! AT&T's benchmarking group estimates that a moderate-sized project takes four to six months and incurs out-of-pocket costs of US$20 000. When personnel costs are included, the figure is easily three to four times higher. But very often, returns on the investment are well worth the effort. Chaparral Steel sends its first-line supervisors on sabbaticals around the globe, where they visit academic and industry leaders, develop an understanding of new work practices and technologies, then bring back what they have learned to the company and apply it to daily operations. As a result, Chaparral is one of the five lowest-cost steel plants in the world.

General Electric's (GE's) impact programme originally sent manufacturing managers to Japan to study factory innovations, such as quality circles and *kanban* cards, and then apply them in their own organizations.

Today Europe is the destination, and productivity improvement practices the target. The programme is one reason GE has recorded productivity gains annually in the last few years.

The final step in benchmarking involves the adaptation, improvement and implementation of appropriate benchmark process enablers. The objective of benchmarking is to change an organization in a way that increases its performance. Thus benchmarking is a process with a built-in bias for action. If you are really serious about benchmarking you must accept the fact that it goes beyond conducting a business process study or obtaining a relative measure of business performance. Like re-engineering or, for that matter, visioning or even training on telephone-handling techniques, do not embark on anything you have no intention of carrying through to fruition! It is not fair to make your people always feel like bridesmaids but never the bride.

Benchmarking was very poorly understood in the beginning. When Xerox first disclosed its existence to the public, journalists likened it to 'industrial espionage'. Xerox was depicted as a business 'spymaster' and the whole practice was regarded as sinister, unacceptable behaviour.

Kent Johnson, corporate counsel for Texas Instruments, said that in those days, when lawyers heard about benchmarking from their corporate clients, their first reaction was to say, 'My God, we've got to tell them not to do this.'

The fundamental distinction between competitive intelligence and benchmarking lies in the degree of openness with which an organization pursues its benchmarking effort. In benchmarking, the objective is to develop an open sharing of information directly with the target company. In this environment, any hint of 'industrial espionage' is eliminated because the investigation is conducted openly rather than in secret.

The American Productivity and Quality Centre's International Benchmarking Clearinghouse addressed this concern by co-operating in the development of a code of conduct for benchmarking with the US Strategic Planning Institute's Council on Benchmarking. This code of conduct is subscribed to by over 100 American companies as the normative behaviour for conducting benchmarking studies. The code describes the protocol of benchmarking – the set of conventions prescribing correct etiquette and procedures to be used in conducting the benchmarking exercise.

The Hong Leong group in Malaysia makes good use of benchmarking. Starting from one small company in 1963, it has mushroomed into a huge diversified conglomerate and is now a leading player in the

Malaysian corporate environment. Its very enlightened chairman feels that if the group does not upgrade its quality systems in order to provide world-class products and services, it will eventually lose its competitiveness. ('World class' is noteworthy – when you benchmark against the best in your industry you are just 'catching-up', but when you benchmark against the best in the world, you are leap-frogging.)

Quality system review

Hong Leong's internal consulting arm, the operations and productivity department, under the capable leadership of Dr Tan Beng Cheok and Chua Jim Boon, started a quality system review for use by every operating company in the group. What is the purpose of the review?

> *To benchmark 'best in class' company performance and compare operating companies' performance in order to drive continuous and breakthrough improvements in Quality, Cost, Delivery, Service and Speed in order to sustain growth and obtain customer delight and loyalty.*

The review is a process whereby operating companies benchmark their quality system in order to ensure their effectiveness in achieving total customer satisfaction. Operating companies in the group assess their current quality systems through benchmarking. Once the assessment is completed, the operating companies will conduct a series of continuous improvement programmes to overcome deficiencies in any of the processes.

To benchmark, operating companies are furnished with guidelines based on a number of key concepts such as:

◆ Quality is defined by the customer. (I have often heard management bragging about how good their companies are; such corporate arrogance is easily deflated by customer feedback. Customers are the only ones who determine if you are truly good.)

◆ Operations and decisions need to be based upon facts and data.

◆ Shorten the response time of all operations and processes.

The quality system review guidelines comprise seven categories that represent the main components of a quality management system:

◆ leadership and entrepreneurship

◆ problem solving and analysis

◆ strategic quality planning

◆ employee involvement and development

◆ products and services innovation

♦ quality results

♦ customer satisfaction.

In order to encourage the group in using the guidelines, a quality award is bestowed each year on the operating company that has satisfied the stringent criteria of the guidelines.

Chapter 5
Operational Diagnosis – Why We Work the Way We Do

At this stage of your re-engineering project, you will need to conduct an operational analysis and a behavioural analysis. These analyses enable you to identify the windows of opportunities for improvement and redesign. In this chapter, we'll talk about operational analysis.

But first, a word of warning. Go-getters have a penchant for action. As a result, one of the most common traps to fall into when embarking on re-engineering is to skip analysis and jump right into redesign. After all, go-getters are used to dealing with the bottom line. However, prescription or treatment is impossible without a diagnosis, no matter how brilliant the physician or consultant. Diagnoses can be very revealing. If you enjoy being in touch with the grassroots, if you enjoy asking questions and looking for information that you have never even considered before, you will delight in the analysis phase of organizational re-engineering.

No organization can re-engineer all its processes simultaneously. Organizations embarking on a comprehensive re-engineering effort often find themselves biting off more than they can chew.

Choosing your processes

So which processes in an organization should be analysed and re-engineered first? Typically, organizations use three criteria to help them make their choices.

The first is dysfunction. Which processes are in the deepest trouble? From the symptoms you see, what diseases do they indicate?

The second is importance. Which processes have the greatest impact on the company's customers?

The third is feasibility. Which of the company's processes are at the moment most susceptible to successful redesign?

Here are some additional questions you may wish to ask yourself:

◆ Which processes consume the largest amount of resources?

◆ Which processes require the longest time?

◆ Which processes have a high number of controls?

◆ Which processes have a high number of manual functions?

◆ Which processes have multiple data entries and pass-offs?

◆ Which processes have a large amount of loop-back and rework?

◆ Which processes have relatively high rates of error?

Generally, the larger a process – the more organizational units it involves – the broader its scope.

Remember you must seek to understand how your current processes work, not analyse them to death. Detailed process analysis of a conventional sort may be useful to help persuade others in your organization (or for consultants to impress clients) that re-engineering is necessary or desirable, but there is no need to continue flogging a dead horse. What you are now looking for is knowledge and insight. So, in that you don't have to collect and analyse volumes of quantitative data, understanding a process is less complex and time-consuming than analysing it. However, it is no less difficult. In fact, in some ways, understanding is harder than analysis.

Understanding your processes

Traditional process analysis takes the process inputs and outputs as given and looks inside the process to measure and examine what goes on. Process understanding, in contrast, takes nothing for granted. A re-engineer attempting to understand a process does not accept the existing output as a given. Part of understanding a process is comprehending what the process 'customer' does with that output. The best place for the re-engineer to begin to understand a process is at the customer end. What are the customers' real requirements? Understanding customer needs is more than just asking customers what they want. They can only say what they think they want. Rather, you have to understand the customers better than they understand themselves. You or your people might actually move in and observe and/or work with customers in their own environments. In re-engineering, when we conduct analyses we do it where it happens! Work is performed where it makes the most sense. What people do and what they say they do are almost never the same.

Process modelling Next you must build a map or model of your current situation.

Process mapping started through:

◆ work study in manufacturing environments in which industrial engineers used scientific methods of observation to collect data for analysis

◆ organization and method studies in which office operations were analysed to achieve accurate manloading (crewing) for optimal utilization of workhours

◆ process control in which the dynamic characteristics of production facilities were analysed as a basis for gathering information and then using the data to control outputs by adjusting inputs to the process

◆ process simulation in which complex processes such as nuclear reactors, chemical plants or highly automated facilities in the engineering industry were modelled on computers to test their response to a wide variety of operating conditions

◆ business modelling as an aid to corporate planning during which business results were predicted in a simulation using mathematical and statistical modelling techniques in order to gain an understanding of the impact of influences such as price, volume, capacity and input costs

◆ systems engineering and analysis in which flow diagrams were used to define the operation of procedures for which the intention was to utilize computers and telecommunications equipment to affect some or all of the process.

A business process model may be defined as a representation of the company's operation or a specific part of the operation. It is usually a graphical depiction of the structure and activities of the operation. The model often shows the relationships between work steps and their sequence. Together these representations portray workflow.

The overall corporate model is usually composed of many individual interrelated models. These models will differ according to the areas they address and the modelling techniques used.

Regardless of the techniques used in the individual models, all the detailed models form an integrated whole. For example, as the flow of an activity leaves one department, it must pick up again in one or more other departments. The ability to track the flow across these boundaries is important. When this can be done, the models are integrated. To accomplish this synergy among models, it is necessary to set standards that direct the manner in which the models will link together.

Typically, a model contains information about each work step and about each aspect of the operation's performance and support. For example, in a company with several locations the model tells what each location does, when it does it, why it does it, and how the action is performed. It also discusses the information services support, all applicable business rules and the interaction with other work steps, work-flows and processes. The relationships between the various locations are also shown, as partially assembled products are sent to other locations for the next step.

To be complete therefore, the model must show all activity and the relationships between:

◆ each department's mission and the activity the department performs

- activities (workflow)

- activities and process

- rules and process

- the department's plan and its processes

- activities and jobs.

Through its supporting information it must answer the questions of who, what, when, where, how and why for each activity. Any outsourced activity should also be described along with its requirements.

There are many organizational modelling tools available. A brief description of some of these tools follows. You may use any of them.

Organizational modelling tools

Tree diagram

In this 'decomposition' technique, a breakdown is shown as limbs from a central trunk. As you go down a limb, it branches to show how something splits into component parts. This branching continues until the desired level of detail is shown. Using this technique, an operation can be repeatedly divided until all tasks are identified. Tree diagrams do not show flow.

Warnier-Orr diagram

Warnier-Orr diagrams are decomposition charts showing the hierarchical structure of business functions or systems. They are laid out horizontally rather than vertically.

State transition diagram

To provide logic for digital processes, a diagram showing processes as a connected network of discrete states is sometimes useful. For this purpose 'states' must be defined for each station in a work process, the two simplest being active and waiting. State transition diagrams are most useful in re-engineering when the process is already heavily automated.

Ishikawa diagram

Like tree diagrams, this technique, sometimes referred to as 'fishbone diagramming', operates using a central process line. Activities are placed along this line as angled intersecting lines.

Hierarchy chart

These models are decomposition diagrams, similar to trees. Beginning with a single global statement of action, they are then broken down (or 'factored' or 'decomposed') into lower levels of detail. The relationship is vertical, showing how actions at each level are divided into components. 'Organigrams' or organization charts are one form of hierarchy charts.

Synaptic model

Synaptic models attempt to simulate the workings of the human brain. They represent a matrix or network view of action. Processes are paths through the model, with the nodes being either activities or organizational units.

Network model

Network models begin with a single starting-point and then show each successive step. Flow is implied by the position of the step. The relationship between the steps is shown by their placement. A commonly used application of a network model is the PERT chart.

Computerized simulation model

A simulation model artificially reproduces the behaviour of a real process. These models are generally computer programs that can be relied on to demonstrate the changed behaviour of a process when key variables are altered. An example is an inventory model, which shows outputs such as inventory levels and costs, given the input of stock withdrawals and replenishment.

Mathematical model

There are several forms of mathematical models, the

most useful of which is linear programming. Linear programmes are a series of simultaneous linear equations, called constraints, and what is known as an objective function, which is another equation that tells the model what the business wants to optimize. For example, a linear programming model may be ingredients for an aftershave lotion. The objective function would be the sum of all of the costs of each ingredient, expressed as the amount used multiplied by the unit price of each, and the constraints would be the upper and lower limits of each ingredient that must be used to make the product.

Action workflow model

A new approach to representing business processes is the development of a new language. Terry Winograd, of Stanford University, and the Action Technologies Company, of Alameda, California, are collaborating on a management technique that has the potential of becoming a breakthrough in most basic workflow management methods and perhaps in the management of work in general. The addition made by this group is that the interactions among the members of a group at work, which have been overlooked or assumed to be a constant factor, are being defined and supported by automation. This approach is beneficial in service workflows, for which the customer can now become part of the model.

Business activity map

Business activity maps (BAMs) are flow diagrams that identify the activities being performed and depict the flow of work and the relationships between activities. They show all decisions and the branching flow paths that result. The antecedents of this type of diagram have been called bubble charts, data flow diagrams, and workflow diagrams.

Relational diagram

Relational diagrams are used to model how a job is performed. This is the first technique that depicts the interaction between a person's activity and the systems of operations supporting it. This interaction is shown as a flow that moves from action to action. As work is performed, the relationships between actions are described.

Flowchart

Flowcharting, one of the oldest forms of work process modelling, is a graphical representation of the sequence of steps in a task or activity. The first step in flowcharting is to define the work steps and their sequence. Next, all decisions and relationships are identified. Finally, the work steps are drawn in a straight-line representation of the flow. Decisions are shown as branching, where one or another choice is made.

Brown paper system explosion

When maintenance and operating workers at Union Carbide's plant in Taft, Louisiana, drew their processes on a huge piece of brown paper (an act referred to as 'system explosion') and then redesigned them, they found savings worth more than US$20 million. Efficiency experts from the early days 'pioneered' the use of brown papers, used for wrapping and packaging – the most easily available papers and found in abundance at manufacturing plants.

In this electronic world of computerized flowcharting, most people are puzzled as to why you should spend time pasting pieces of brown paper together to form one large piece and then drawing a flow on it. It seems a somewhat primitive way of doing things. There are many good reasons for using a brown paper.

First, because of its size, not only can you capture a flow of a process, but you will also have the room to stick copies of all the pieces of paperwork involved in a process on to the brown paper.

Second, by having the process owner 'construct' the brown paper with you and then soliciting his opinion on the weaknesses of the process, and the windows of opportunities for improvement, you are involved in a buy-in or ownership process. What is actually happening is that you are getting the process owner to critique the process him or herself. As you redesign the process together later, he or she will feel part of the solution and will therefore not sit back and criticize.

Third, because of its size, a brown paper is a dramatic and very explicit and graphical selling tool. I have seen brown papers many times the size of the wall of a typical boardroom. Often as I unroll the brown paper, I hear chief executives sighing or exclaiming and making comments like 'My goodness, is this how our processes work? No wonder we are not making money!'

Many of my re-engineering projects were started on the strength of the brown paper presentations. Such an enormous and vivid pictorial portrayal of a company's gargantuan and often illogical processes is reason enough to 'kick start' chief executives of organizations into re-engineering. In fact, I once had a chief executive who was so affected by what he saw that he suffered a heart attack in the middle of a brown paper presentation. In case you are wondering, we did do a project – when he recovered, one of the first things he did was to make sure that the re-engineering project was begun.

Chapter 6
Behavioural Analysis – the Touchy Feely Stuff

Having conducted an operational analysis, your next task is to understand the human side of enterprise, the behavioural analysis.

In Chapter 1 we mentioned that once a go-getting norm pervades an organization, great and wonderful things can happen.

Norms can best be diagnosed through what I call 'heart-beat' studies – surveys to determine the burning issues existing within an organization. These may take the form of predesigned surveys or you may design your own questionnaire. One key point to remember is that to achieve the best result from such surveys, and to solicit frank feedback, you should insist on anonymity and confidentiality. In other words, do not ask respondents to state their names.

Another important point is to be sensitive about the questions you ask. Try not to ask questions on issues which you have no desire to, or are not in a position to, change.

When the news organization Reuters conducted its climate survey in 1992 with my assistance, it had already decided to move from Raffles Place to Science Park. At that time, its multi-million dollar building was near completion at Science Park. There were some 'murmurs' from a few employees who preferred to work in the city than in Science Park, which is in the suburbs. But the decision to move was firm, the building was about to be completed. Nothing anybody said would make Reuters change its mind about moving to Science Park, so in the climate survey questionnaire we took care not to ask questions like 'What do you think about the move to Science Park?'

A carefully constructed questionnaire will enable you to determine the main topics of the day – are people unhappy with the recent change in medical insurance coverage; has the company been organizing enough social activities for its staff in the last several months; does the food served by the new canteen operator live up to expectations? Addressing these equally important concerns turns attention away from the unwelcome move and establishes a positive problem-solving image for the management, boosting morale all round.

Dow Corning project I conducted a heart-beat study for American chemical multinational Dow Corning which enabled management to understand how employees felt about work, about fellow employees and about the organization. Based on the findings, a project was designed to address issues causing concern within the organization, particularly in the area of customer service procedures and systems. Because much excitement was generated, responses to the study were honest and frank and management was equally sincere in wanting to re-engineer the organization for optimal effectiveness and to grant employees a quality work life. The project won support all round. Well-established and archaic norms were destroyed. New ways of working were engineered and behaviour change started, leading to a happier working atmosphere.

Once positive go-getting norms pervade an organization, great and wonderful things can indeed take place. Properly handled, norms can be effective change agents, triggering off a series of positive organizational behavioural patterns that in turn become desired norms.

Let us go through the process used in the Dow Corning case. I first talked to a few key Dow Corning clients, using a questionnaire as a guide.

Questionnaire to Dow Corning clients

1   I am a consultant engaged by Dow Corning to improve their customer service. What is your general feeling about Dow Corning's customer service?

2   If you were running Dow Corning, what would you change? Why?

3   What other areas could be improved upon?

4   What is the worst part of dealing with Dow Corning?

5   What do they do well?

I next conducted four focus group meetings with all Dow Corning employees.

Questionnaire to Dow Corning focus groups

1   I am a consultant engaged by your company to provide customer service and team-building training. What is your general feeling about Dow Corning's customer service?

2   If you were running Dow Corning, what would you change? Why?

3   What other areas could be improved upon?

4   What is the worst part of working here?

The findings were very revealing. Bear in mind that these are only the perceptions of the people surveyed and may not be facts. However, very often a person's perception becomes his or her reality. Re-engineering offers an opportunity to set things right and to correct misperceptions and misconceived ideas. Some of the responses show discontent among the staff:

1   I am a consultant engaged by your company to provide customer service and team-building training. What is your general feeling about Dow Corning's customer service?

'Problematic – procedures do not make sense.'
'People not co-operating.'
'Not co-ordinated for customer service.'

'Customers are pushed around.'
'Roles not clear cut.'
'Not motivated to act as a team.'

2   If you were running Dow Corning, what would you change? Why?

'Assess situation – if there are human relations problems management has to do something.'
'Transfer some people away.'
'We need more definitive job descriptions.'
'Supervisors should talk to under-performers and give them 6 months to improve.'
'The job descriptions are too vague and general.'

3   What other areas could be improved upon?

'Staff should be informed of changes in the office that the management know are going to affect everyone, e.g. the new telephone system. Also, one day we came in and the old fax machine had been taken away and a new one installed. This affects me.'
'We should be informed of everything. If someone quits, they just disappear – no one knows. Who's going to do his job then?'
'We need someone to take care of benefits and company policies.'
'There is a set of company policy criteria but I had to get it from someone else.'
'There should be training for employees. I wanted training on MS Word but nothing was done. I was kind of disappointed actually.'

4   What is the worst part of working here?

'Long hours.'

'Lots of OT without OT pay.'

'I work late because I have too much to do. Our procedures are a burden to me.'

'We only get an extra month's pay at year end, nothing more.'

'We're not motivated to give our best because everyone gets the same pay so why bother? It's not according to performance.'

'A lot of people are fed up with the telephone system.'

Heart-beat study for Dow Corning

I then conducted a heart-beat study using this questionnaire:

A Kindly tick [ ] what you feel are relevant statements.

B Spontaneity and speed assure accuracy. Do not ponder.

C Your name is *not* required.

D When completed, fold paper in half and hand it to me.

1 The physical arrangements at work are unsatisfactory. [ ]

2 People are discontented with the pay and benefits. [ ]

3 I do not feel secure about my job. [ ]

4 Dow Corning has not greatly helped my personal development. [ ]

5   Top management is not concerned with my views. [ ]

6   I have little real interest in my job. [ ]

7   The work environment is depressing. [ ]

8   Policy on leave is below standard. [ ]

9   I have doubts about my long-term security. [ ]

10 Most people here have little opportunity to gain new experience. [ ]

11 I would like to be consulted more when decisions are made. [ ]

12 My job has no clear targets. [ ]

13 The colour schemes, lighting and general decor are not good. [ ]

14 The medical and insurance benefits provide unsatisfactory protection. [ ]

15 A number of people are worried about the possibility of retrenchment. [ ]

16 I would like more feedback about my performance. [ ]

17 Employees know too little about Dow Corning aims and plans. [ ]

18 I would benefit from greater challenges in my job. [ ]

19 Dow Corning does not try to develop jobs to fit individual needs. [ ]

20 Dow Corning makes few worthwhile efforts to provide social functions. [ ]

21 Bad employee relations cause major upheavals at times. [ ]

22 My training has rarely been well planned. [ ]

23 There is no systematic effort to identify employees' views. [ ]

24 I am not given new responsibilities, even though I could handle them. [ ]

25 The workplace is poorly cleaned and maintained. [ ]

26 The pay is generally thought to be unfair. [ ]

27 Product competitiveness is poor, affecting the company's long-term prospects. [ ]

28 I should like to have a clearer personal development plan. [ ]

29 Most people feel uninvolved in decision making. [ ]

30 My job no longer presents a challenge to me. [ ]

31 Places for lunch are not good. [ ]

32 Total remuneration package does not compare favourably with similar firms. [ ]

33 If I were to leave, Dow Corning would not miss my contributions. [ ]

34 Insufficient effort is put into developing people's skills. [ ]

35 Managers and workers should have closer links. [ ]

36 I am often bored at work. [ ]

How I feel about working at Dow Corning. (Please write in capitals. Management will not read this. Management will only read a summary of all the employees' comments.)

Space was then allowed for employees' comments.

Statements 1, 7, 13, 19, 25 and 31 are related to work environment; statements 2, 8, 14, 20, 26 and 32 to remuneration; statements 3, 9, 15, 21, 27 and 33 to security; statements 4, 10, 16, 22, 28 and 34 to personal development; statements 5, 11, 17, 23, 29 and 35 to involvement, and statements 6, 12, 18, 24, 30 and 36 to work-related interest and challenge. Figure 6.1 depicts the frequency of mention among the four focus groups of employees. The findings reveal that most employees are not motivated by what they perceive to be a lack of personal development. They would also like management to adopt a more participative management style. (During the project and when I re-engineered the company, I was careful to bear these concerns in mind.)

I summarized the findings in one page and submitted it to David Cave, region manager (Singapore, Malaysia, Indonesia, Philippines) of Dow Corning – effectively the top man in charge of the company in the region. Some of the comments in the summary included:

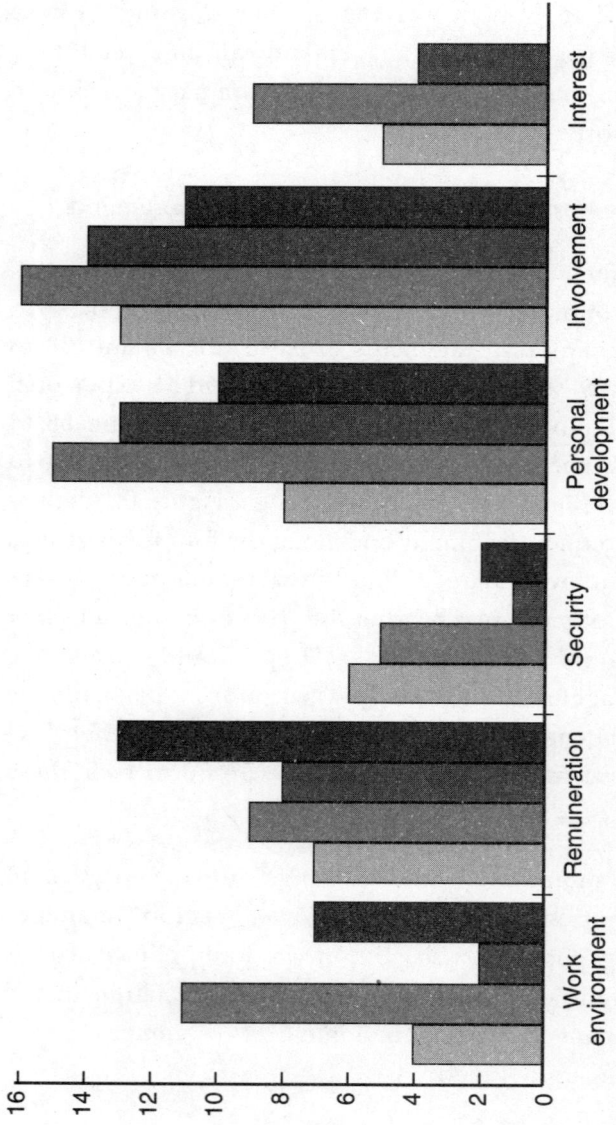

Figure 6.1   Heart-beat study for Dow Corning, 1994

The seven clients interviewed by the consultant expressed no great concern regarding Dow Corning's service except for the hang-ups with wanting better predictability over shipping schedules.

I also rang Dow Corning 16 times and found no serious blunder in the way telephone calls are handled. The telephone handling was not fantastic but nothing critical was detected.

The four focus group meetings revealed insufficient co-operation among colleagues, a desire to have advance notice of management decisions and frustration with the telephone system.

The heart-beat study revealed nothing adverse as far as the organizational climate is concerned. Employee perception indicated a desire for more company-sponsored training and participative management.

Nothing beats a questionnaire which is custom-designed for the specific situation but if expertise in that is lacking there are predesigned generic questionnaires and 'instrumentation' available from organizations specializing in such measurement.

Chapter 7
Leadership and Power – Who's Who in Your Organization

A successful re-engineering project is highly dependent on strong leadership within the organization. This issue will be addressed in this chapter by taking another detour.

During the early 1990s Kodak, IBM, American Express and General Motors sacked their CEOs. All were outstanding business leaders and models of competency with impressive track records. All had promised turn-rounds and all had spearheaded strategic cost reduction, productivity improvement and organizational effectiveness programmes to deliver those promises. Indeed most of these efforts paid off, at least in the beginning. Yet despite this frenzy of activity, the competitive edge of these companies continued to ebb away until finally their boards had to act.

What went wrong? The answer is leadership, or lack of it.

Whether an organization is large or small, or presided over by a tyrant or someone who acts as if he or she has studied non-directive techniques under a Zen master, it is to one degree or another an exercise in collaborative management. Modern organizations are much too complex to be run by one person in isolation.

Group approaches to problem solving and decision making are here to stay. Contrary to what many westerners might think about the participation or consensus style of management practised in Japan, disagreement is allowed. At Honda for example, any employee can call for a *waigaya* session during which people lay their cards on the table and confront problems face to face. Neither groups nor individuals are bad *per se*. The problem is that bad groups and individuals are bad. And it's the leaders who allow them to go bad.

Take the case of this service organization. The managing director, to all intents and purposes, has long ago 'relinquished' his power to a trusted 'internal consultant', a subordinate who has wormed his way into the managing director's heart.

The situation is not unlike that created by the new CEO of IBM, Louis Gerstner. The *Wall Street Journal* reports on Gerstner's continuous blind faith in two staffers, Bernard Puckett and Ned Lautenbach, both of whom have failed dismally in the past. Puckett, who is Gerstner's 'strategist', was in charge of IBM's mainframe business in 1990 and ran it on a strategy that had it falling apart in 1991. Lautenbach still runs IBM's huge overseas operations, even though he failed through a series of jobs in the 1980s and presided over IBM's Asian operations while they fell into disarray in the early 1990s.

The 'internal consultant' in our story has never been to school but has manoeuvred himself into a powerful position and has manipulated the young and inexperienced boss into eating out of his hands. The managing director spends several hours a day with this predator who has, since joining the organization, advised his boss to remove two of his peers, on the basis that they were 'undesirable'. However, now that these undesirables have been removed, the company has yet to turn around. What is sad is that the boss knows no better. Day after day he is under the sway of his 'internal consultant'. Unhappy colleagues have also started quitting. Some members of the staff conducted an independent investigation of the man in question and found that he has a bad reputation; he is a gambler, a womanizer and an alcoholic, and he has a track record of failing whenever teamwork is required. So his *modus operandi* in every company he works at is to position himself as 'adviser' to the boss. Concerned parties eventually warned the boss about this person but he refused to believe them, saying that this man 'adds value' with his information and advice. So our 'internal consultant', wallowing in the comfort offered by his vantage spot, like a buffoon on a perch, ultimately assisted the boss in destroying the organization.

One wonders if lunacy and leadership share certain characteristics. A neurotic leader can accelerate his organization's downfall and make it crumble in no time. A superb example of this can be found in the person of J. Edgar Hoover.

From 1924 until his death in 1972, J. Edgar Hoover dominated the Federal Bureau of Investigation with his deep suspicion, hypersensitivity, and never-ending readiness to repel any threats to his authority. The FBI under Hoover became less an agency for diplomatic detective work than a crime-related war department, an entity all its own, complete with battle strategies, secret campaigns and refined intelligence system.

Unlike our managing director friend, Hoover had no need for someone to whisper poison into his ears. He started it all himself. The FBI had been vigorous and aggressive even before he became director, rounding up draft dodgers after the First World War, breaking strikes and Ku-Klux-Klan rallies during the Harding administration, and compiling dossiers on over 200 000 'suspected communists' in the early 1920s. But it was still Hoover, as the bureau's assistant director, who had overseen these operations in those early days. In fact Harding's attorney-general, A. Mitchell Palmer, was eventually to comment on how impressed he'd become with young Hoover's 'great zeal' and 'distrust'. As the years went by, over a career that spanned nine presidential administrations and almost fifty years, this same zeal and consummate distrust were to become both the bureau's and Hoover's trade marks.

Hoover was finicky about violations of even the most trifling rules and regulations. Slight errors or off-the-cuff remarks could cause an agent's transfer, suspension or firing without warning.

One former agent recounts a story of Hoover being driven through the streets of Washington in his limousine. Another vehicle suddenly banged into the left side of his car as both tried to make a left turn. From that moment on, Hoover never again sat behind his driver. He ordered that henceforth there would be 'no left turns' taken at any time when he was a passenger. Movements to the left, he decreed, must be made by turning right, then right again, right once more, then proceeding two blocks down to the street in question and turning right once again.

When Hoover overheard a TWA pilot criticize the FBI's handling of a hijack case, he issued an official directive forbidding all bureau agents to fly TWA. He dispatched a similar order, too, regarding Xerox after being angered by their lack of co-operation during the investigation of a case. Xerox machines were subsequently removed from all bureau offices.

Leaders like Hoover and our managing director friend create an atmosphere of distrust in an organization. Their behaviour inevitably breeds feelings of insecurity and disenchantment and a high staff turnover may result.

Someone once defined insanity as doing the same thing again and again but expecting different results. *Doing* is the assumed managerial constant. To manage is to *do* something; managers are selected and promoted on their ability to get things done. But management differs from leadership. The Japanese chart the journey across life in terms of perfecting one's inner nature, or being. They call it *kokoro*. By contrast, the rest of us typically assess our progression through life in terms of personal wealth or number of acquisitions – the house we live in, the car we drive, the breed of pet dogs we keep, the destination of our holidays, *ad nauseam*. To the Japanese, merely *doing* these things is meaningless unless one is able to become deeper and wiser along the way.

What sort of a leader will pave the path for the success of a re-engineering project?

It has been said that if you want a pet, you should buy a dog. A leader should not practise favouritism. He or she should be impartial, open to new ideas, a visionary, inspiring the masses and providing them with support and encouragement. He or she should allow people to realize their potential. Above all, a leader should be a synergizer and a harmonizer, orchestrating resources and motivating people to pull together for the common good, and become deeper and wiser along the way. Blessed is such a transformational leader, for re-engineering success shall be his or hers.

Transformational leadership is a concept opposite to that of transactional leadership. It has the following dimensions:

Transforma-tional leadership

◆ charismatic behaviour

◆ individualized consideration

◆ intellectual stimulation

leading to performance beyond expectations from subordinates.

Charismatic behaviour

How would you feel about placing an ageing, overweight manager with a hair-trigger temper and a thick skin for criticism in charge of one of the most complex organizations ever created?

Many observers were openly critical of George Bush's appointment of General H. Norman Schwarzkopf as commander-in-chief of allied military operations during the Gulf War. Much of their criticism was based on the precise traits noted above.

In retrospect, however, Schwarzkopf proved to be the perfect choice for the job. He adroitly handled a military force composed of armies from dozens of different cultures. His subordinates placed their complete faith in his abilities and decisions. He justified their trust by plotting a truly brilliant military campaign. And the media grew to respect Schwarzkopf as a compassionate, down-to-earth and honest leader.

After the surprisingly easy military victory in early 1991, popular opinion of many American leaders – George Bush and James Baker, for example – skyrocketed. But Schwarzkopf's star was among the brightest. In his home state of Florida a grassroots movement to draft him as senatorial candidate was started and many American business leaders stated that Schwarzkopf would be a marvellous CEO or director.

What qualities led to his enormous appeal? One was the high quality of his decision making. Another was the fact that he was genuinely concerned about the human life that was involved on both sides of the conflict. Finally, Schwarzkopf was a great communicator who presented the facts in a simple, occasionally humorous, and always direct way. He was charismatic.

Charisma is a form of interpersonal attraction that inspires support and acceptance. The following characteristics are believed to contribute to charisma:

◆ The followers trust the correctness of the leader's beliefs.

◆ The followers' beliefs are similar to the leader's beliefs.

◆ The followers accept the leader unquestioningly.

◆ The followers feel affection for the leader.

◆ The followers obey the leaders willingly.

◆ The followers have an emotional involvement in the organization's mission.

◆ The followers have heightened performance goals.

◆ The followers believe they can contribute to the success of the group's goals.

Charismatic behaviour instils pride, faith and respect, and conveys a sense of vision. Another illustration of this kind of behaviour is where Cray Research disregarded Steven Chin's plea to build a supercomputer and 40 colleagues followed him out the door after he told them that his vision of a supercomputer must be built because 'the future of technology in this country [USA] is at stake'.

Individualized consideration

Individualized consideration delegates tasks to stimulate learning, emphasizes the individual needs of each subordinate and is based on respecting each as an individual.

Intellectual stimulation

Intellectual stimulation introduces and encourages developing new ideas and rethinking old ones with an emphasis on the many angles in performing a job.

Transformational leadership broadens and elevates the goals of subordinates and gives them confidence to go beyond their expectations.

Transactional leadership, on the other hand, involves daily exchanges between leaders and subordinates and is necessary for routine performance agreed upon between leaders and subordinates. These exchanges involve contingent rewards and management by exception. In essence, contingent rewards are provided in exchange for mutually agreed upon performance accomplishment. Management by exception involves leaving subordinates alone if the old ways are working or if subordinates are meeting mutually accepted performance goals.

This form of leadership may be appropriate for

effective daily performance. However, transformational leadership is needed to go beyond this routine accomplishment.

Related to the issue of leadership is the issue of power. Power is the potential ability of a person or group to influence another person or group. The key words here are 'potential ability' – a power person need not even act – based on the possibility that he can act in an impactful manner, he becomes powerful.

Power

Generally six bases of power can exist in organizations:

1   Expert power – the extent to which a person controls technical expertise that is valuable to someone else.

2   Legitimate power – granted by virtue of one's position in the organization.

3   Coercive power – the extent to which a person has the ability to punish or physically or psychologically harm someone else.

4   Reward power – the extent to which a person controls rewards that another person values.

5   Referent power – when one person wants to be liked or imitates someone else who is perceived to possess power.

6   Information power – when a person is powerful due to the information he or she possesses.

An effective leader should be able to use a

combination of these forms of power for their own advantage and for the good of their organization.

It is also useful during a meeting, especially in the early stages of a re-engineering project, if you can determine who your allies are; who the project's supporters are – separating the dragons from the aimers in the leadership team. By the way the various executives behave, from the questions they ask, the way they use power and the manner in which they try to exert influence it is easy to tell who's who. Dragons are executives who oppose the project for one reason or another, those resistant to change and very often people with *d*irty *r*otten *a*ttitudes *g*oing *o*n *n*evertheless. Aimers are those who aim for the project's success and will work with you to bring about results. Once you have identified the dragons, communicate with them, spend time talking to them, address their concerns – which are usually no more than misperceptions about re-engineering – and involve them with hands-on work. Like Paul on the road to Damascus, a converted dragon can turn out to be your greatest champion.

Chapter 8
A Fish Rots from the Head

Companies are learning that simply reducing staff numbers, rather than reorganizing the way people in different functions work, won't yield quantum leaps in performance, and reorganizing the way people work is not possible without a basic understanding of how change affects people. The best way to show your concern for people is to lead by example. In Japanese companies change almost always begins at the top. Corporate executives cannot be change leaders until they have committed to change themselves. This is more than just paying lip-service to change. Once a top executive has intellectually accepted the need for change, his or her heart and soul must follow. And then the leader must win the heart, soul, and intellect of every member of the organization.

Owing to the dramatic impact re-engineering has on the organization and its business, leaders cannot 'delegate' re-engineering to someone else within the organization. Re-engineering demands more day-to-day involvement on the part of senior executives than any other effort, which leaders can 'kick off' and then delegate and leverage.

Some senior executives simply don't know how to sponsor a re-engineering project. What is top management support? What actions and behaviours are required? What messages should they relay throughout the organization?

Sometimes education is the problem. Executives don't understand what re-engineering is and therefore apply the term loosely. Many executives still confuse re-engineering with the more gradual and incremental approach of process improvement.

The best defence is offence. Incorporate the following activities in your re-engineering project plan.

◆ Manage expectations. Few business executives are pessimists. Most tend to be enthusiastic optimists who believe that almost anything is possible. This positive predisposition can, however, lead to runaway expectations for the re-engineering project. Do not deny the complexity of the effort. Do not forget the fact that fundamental change takes time and requires continual training and support. Do not confuse your vision with the reality of making the vision happen. Remind yourself that seeing it in your mind doesn't make it real, and that much work must be done to make it so. Executives who are used to being rewarded for short-term performance will always push for short-term results. This creates a very short attention span that demands quick fixes. A re-engineering project typically takes 12 to 18 months to deliver its first benefits, and the pain of change becomes more intense as people try to let go of old habits and assimilate new ideas and knowledge. The ambiguity and dysfunction of this transition is not easy for an executive used to quick fixes.

◆ Communicate. It is impossible to over-communicate. Simplify your message, no matter how complex the issue. Anticipate the issues, and communicate your position early. The change leader must communicate the compelling need for the change being contemplated, as well as the vision he or she has set out for the company's future state. When a leader shows the organization the urgency of working differently, even when the change itself involves pain, change is more readily accepted.

IBM's CEO, Louis Gerstner, believes that 'selling' the new IBM culture to the worldwide enterprise is a fundamental aspect of his job. Since becoming CEO in 1993, Gerstner has travelled extensively, talking to IBM employees and customers. In a typical week, Gerstner's schedule includes trips to Atlanta, Orlando, and Helsinki, Finland, to explain and promote the new ways of doing business.

Gerstner believes changes must be sold by the chief executive face to face. 'It's not something you do by writing memos,' he says. 'You've got to appeal to people's emotions. They've got to buy in with their hearts and their bellies, not just their minds.'

Face-to-face communication, even if not one on one, is important because of the opportunity for interaction. This give and take, called active communication, is far more apt to achieve buy-in than passive communications, such as memos.

Active communication also enables you to keep your eyes and ears open and to look out for patterns of behaviour that indicate a person has a need for control or a secret, self-centred agenda. In re-engineering, acts of sabotage do not take the form of land mines or cut telephone lines. Political attacks, passive aggressive behaviour, and unpredictable acts more accurately describe re-engineering terrorism and sabotage. Corporate terrorists and saboteurs attack, either overtly, covertly or both, when the project does not take a direction that suits them.

If you know of such a person, directly confront the offender privately. Describe the unacceptable behaviour and explain how it affects the project. Offer to help and jointly develop a plan for proceeding in which the person accepts responsibility for his or her behaviour.

If the behaviour persists, move the person out of the project if possible. If the person cannot be moved for one reason or another, strengthen the team's work, roles and relationships. 'Damage control' – carefully plan the project to minimize terrorist and saboteur activity.

Transforming an organization is not an easy task. When you re-engineer, you're asking people to change the way they do things. You're also asking them to change their values and their beliefs. This is like trying to wean them off an addiction. An organization comprises people who collectively create the organization's character. Organizations have a tremendous amount of inertia and resist change much more strongly than any one individual within the organization. Not understanding the psychology and sociology of organizations has been the downfall of many re-engineering projects.

Do not make the fatal mistake of thinking that implementation is simple. Tweaking a few processes superficially will not produce significant improvements. Be realistic about how long it takes for change to take place.

Learn to listen and ask questions rather than tell everyone what they should do, feel and expect. Fine-tune project team communication skills, at the heart of which are consulting and selling skills. People up, across and down the organization must be taught what the project team knows. The need-to-know basis of communication is out of date – people deserve to be informed.

The project team should involve everyone they can in the project. They should be willing to 'cry for help' when unforeseen problems and issues arise.

The project team should concentrate on how its members work as intently as on what they accomplish, remembering to model the behaviours appropriate for the re-engineered environment. They must critically review their progress and be able to self-correct as the implementation gets under way. Team members ought to exemplify determination and patience. When complaints are received, the team should view these complaints as appeals for information, understanding and support. The team must help others overcome the anguish of change.

Successful re-engineering demands a broad array of skills and aptitudes. It requires extensive operational experiences and excellent communication skills. The project team must communicate effectively with all levels of the organization, from senior management to front-line staff. Its members should be conversant with both business and technology.

Not many people possess this broad a range of skills. Within any company, there will be relatively few and they will invariably be among the company's most valued employees. Valuing these employees' contributions to day-to-day operations, companies may not be willing to spare these resources. Re-engineering, however, is intensive and difficult, and companies must be willing to apply all the talent at their disposal.

As the organization embarks on re-engineering, do not abandon Total Quality Management (TQM). Re-engineering complements TQM but does not replace it. For badly functioning processes, re-engineer first, then follow with TQM methods to continuously improve the process.

Many companies think that re-engineering is just another term for TQM. It is not. Total Quality Management seeks incremental improvements; re-engineering looks for quantum leaps in performance. The former is improving something that is basically OK; the latter is about taking something that is irrelevant, throwing it out and starting again. Total Quality Management relies on bottom-up, participative decision making in both the planning of a TQM programme and its execution. Re-engineering, on the other hand, is initially driven by top management. When re-engineering is complete, the workplace is largely self-managed, but getting there is sometimes achieved through what may appear to be a very autocratic, non-democratic process. A strong, inspiring leader has to exercise his or her prerogative as the head of the organization, stand up in front of everybody, wave the flag and say, 'Hey, let's do it !' You can't have a weak, indecisive person going around asking, hesitatingly, 'We may have to do some re-engineering, what do you guys think?' Despite our exhortations to be sensitive to the people factor, re-engineering just can't be done that way!

A fish rots from the head. Deming once said that 80 per cent of the problems in an organization begin at the top. If the man or woman at the helm of the organization does not champion re-engineering, nothing substantial will happen. It begins at the top! People at the top must show that they too walk the talk and are willing to take their own medicine. Senior management must exhibit absolute commitment to re-engineering and lead by example.

Part III
STEP THREE

Redesigning, Building and Implementing

Chapter 9
Creativity – Going Where No One Has Gone Before

Creativity is one vital ingredient for successful redesign of processes. In this chapter we make yet another detour to look at how creativity can benefit re-engineering, especially when it comes to redesigning.

In general, any problem-solving situation can be described as a balance between two types of forces – driving forces prompting change and restraining forces resisting change.

Where a complex problem needs to be solved, the first thing to do is to identify the forces on both sides. Then they must be weighed in terms of the amount of force they exert. When we can see more clearly what these various forces are and how significant or strong they are, there is a better chance of bringing about change in the direction we seek.

Change can be brought about in two ways: by increasing the forces prompting change or by reducing the forces resisting change. The most effective way is to add to the driving forces and, at the same time, to weaken the resisting forces. This is where creativity comes in – new ideas are needed here.

But before we look more closely at creativity, let's examine a typical problem-solving process, such as the one used by Xerox:

1   Identify the dysfunction – what do we want to change?

2   Analyse the problem – what's preventing us from reaching the desired state?

3   Generate potential solutions – how could we make the change?

4   Select and plan the solution – what's the best way to do it?

5   Implement the solution – are we following the plan?

6   Evaluate the solution – how well did it work?

Creativity is needed at step 3 – generating potential solutions. If you regard the very first idea that comes to your mind as *the* solution to your problem you are likely to deny yourself the benefits of other potentially better solutions. In the same way, when redesigning processes, be mindful of the fact that the first redesign you have created may not necessarily be the best. Remember – do not take the first redesigned model as final.

That's the trouble with most of us. We do not explore possible solutions enough. However, this is not because we are reluctant to do it, but because we lack the creativity to generate an abundance of possible solutions. So we go through life with second-best alternatives.

Creativity is needed when you have studied the weaknesses of a process and must find windows of opportunities and ways and means to redesign that process. Is creativity an inborn trait or is it a competency which can be acquired?

I believe creativity is a mindset which can be inculcated. To do that we must remove certain assumptions and blockages most of us possess regarding our own ability to be creative. The worst thing is to say to yourself: 'I am not creative' or 'I am not the creative type', as if creativity is exclusive only to certain industries or professions – advertising, architecture, interior design, etc.

How often have you said 'I am not creative'? This is another of those defeating 'chloroform' phrases that knocks people out and reduces them to losers. This self-fulfilling prophecy immediately locks your mind in a deep freeze. You refuse to look beyond possibilities and are constrained by self-imposed limitations. You arrive at a stage where you become 'too lazy to think'. Overdependence on others can lead to that. To move ahead, one must 'grab the bull by its horns'.

Creative thinking, broadly defined, means envisaging something new. It is part of re-engineering.

In 1977, King Taufaahau Topou IV of Tonga faced a problem: in spite of the fact that one of his subjects' prized national foods was fruit bats, there were too many of them and they were destroying crops, reducing the kingdom's exports. The king paid a visit to nearby Guam and set up a sales force to boost Guam's consumption of fruit bats. This increased Tonga's exports and eliminated a lot of bats. The king had found a creative solution!

Creativity has been defined in different ways. Edward Land, the Polaroid inventor, described it as 'the sudden cessation of stupidity' and anthropologist Margaret Mead said, 'To the extent that a person makes, invents or thinks something that is new to him, he may be said to have performed a creative act.'

Japanese philosopher Masatoshi Yoshimura once said, 'Failure to use such an abundant inherent treasure as creativity, whether it be because of unawareness that it exists, indifference, or deliberate stultification, is more than a waste; it is self-betrayal.'

Consider this parable from India. A constant source of mystery for dragonfly nymphs in a pond is what happens to them when, on reaching the age of chrysalis, they pass through the surface of the pond never to return. Each nymph, as it feels impelled to break through the pond's surface, promises to return and tell those who remain behind what really happens, and to confirm or deny a rumour attributed to a frog that when a larva emerges on the other side of the world, it becomes a marvellous creature with a long slender body and iridescent wings. But on emerging from the surface of the pond as a fully formed dragonfly, the transformed nymph is unable to penetrate the surface no matter how much it tries and how long it hovers. The nymphs left behind can only lament: 'Will none of you in pity to those you left behind disclose the secret?'

Like the dragonfly nymphs, we tend to see any act that transforms something old into something new as a *fait accompli* – a finished product that appears as if by magic. We are delighted with the results but feel no obligation to duplicate or even understand them. After all, the whole exercise has taken place outside our natural element. How could we be expected to understand? It is a surprise, an accident.

Instead of viewing creativity as an accident, we should see it as a process – a logical progression of ideas and mental images that can transform the elements of reality into something new. We must dismiss once and for all the myth that creative people are geniuses and that only geniuses are creative. We do expect geniuses to have talent, ability, intelligence, alertness and perseverance. We are also inclined to think that if we do not have these desirable qualities to a high degree we cannot be creative.

The famous Irish writer James Joyce, concerned

about his daughter who was schizophrenic, consulted Swiss psychoanalyst Carl Jung. Jung described the daughter's rambling as free access to her unconscious mind. Joyce was famous for his stream-of-consciousness technique in which he tried to blend subjective and objective reality. Aware that many considered his books as nothing more than the ranting of a madman, he wondered aloud what the difference was between his own and his daughter's use of words. Jung replied, 'You mastered the intellectual dive, she falls'.

Most of us, through lack of understanding and disuse, have permitted our creative thinking skills to fall. As with James Joyce, we can guide and control these skills to utilize the creative process fully.

One way to improve is to re-create your childhood creative thinking skills. Be spontaneous, for example. Aldous Huxley said that a childlike man is not a man whose development has been arrested; on the contrary, he is a man who has given himself a chance of continuing to develop long after most adults have muffled themselves in the cocoon of middle-age habit and convention.

If you think you have reached a plateau where creativity no longer seems possible, it may be because you have unwittingly imposed limits on the skills that make up your point of view. A great paradox of creative thinking is that, when you have discovered a mental combination of structure, order and relation and have identified a pattern for the first time, thereafter each time you use an exact duplication of that pattern, you run the risk of its becoming less creative in coping with fresh experiences. Some things are clever only the first time. This happened to Henry Ford. He introduced the Model T in 1908 and continued to turn out the same car until 1927. (He is supposed to have said the customer could have any colour he wanted, so long as it was black.) The Ford Motor Company lost its pre-eminence because of this stubborn adherence to a once creative idea.

Gertrude Stein had a remarkable ability to make profound statements with deceptive simplicity. Her constant companion Alice Toklas recorded Stein's dying words: 'What is the answer?' Toklas was silent. Stein then asked, 'In that case, what is the question?'

If you are seeking a creative answer to your problem, you must first give sufficient attention to understanding what the problem is. The mind grasps the reality of an experience by structuring, ordering and relating it. Again, these terms are interdependent. We can no more see structure or order or relation separately than we can see only one of the three dimensions. However, without intellectually understanding each one, deeper perspective is lost.

George Bernard Shaw said, 'Some men see things as

they are and ask "Why?" I see them as they have never been and ask "Why not?"'

You can increase your creativity level by interchanging structure, order and relation. A motorist driving a car is an example of this. His situation is constantly changing. As time passes, his location changes. He recognizes on a macrovisual level that his state is constantly changing. As he looks ahead, he sees other cars in relation to him constantly changing. The cars are moving along the highway to the distant horizon. If he thinks creatively, the fact that when his *structure* (car) reaches the distant point of the highway, the *relations* (conditions) that those other cars are now experiencing will be the experience that he *will be* having in a short time. He sees a possible *order* before it happens. He therefore in essence looks into a future time frame. With this realization of order he can change lanes, noting that far ahead one lane is moving faster than another.

From the advertising industry comes A.F. Osborne's brainstorming (free flow listing and eventual selection of ideas) another technique to generate creative ideas and from William Gordon comes the method known as synectics – the joining together of different and apparently irrelevant elements – a process which produces fresh ideas.

When you redesign a process, ask yourself if you

have exhausted all your options. Have you used creative techniques to generate enough redesign options and alternatives? Could better and more effective redesigns be created?

Chapter 10
Re-engineering and Human Resources – the Minds Behind the Warm Bodies

When you re-engineer your organization, the human resource needs of your organization will be changed. This chapter makes our last detour to examine how re-engineering impacts on human resource management.

'Re-engineering' is a term which originated from the world of information technology (IT). Not surprisingly consultants dabbling in the subject have all but neglected the human side of enterprise. For any business, success greatly depends on the performance of its human resources (HR). While it is unusual to find organizations that do not have in their rank and file certain people who take more than they contribute, few can afford to put up with more than a handful of such people and hope to continue for long. There are no cases when one poor performer does not somehow affect the performance of an entire group. If business relies on performance, then so does re-engineering. A re-engineered organization may be even more dependent on everyone in it performing the work for which he or she is ultimately accountable.

Assumptions about personnel management are still loaded with emotions. It is typical of management to assume that each job is critical and to consider it a personal challenge for each manager to squeeze as much as possible out of every worker. Yet managers are told that it is impossible to expect 100 per cent from either the workforce or any individual on a consistent basis. Certain behaviours result from such a mentality. Workers call management hypocrites because management is hanging up posters saying that people are their most precious asset, blah, blah, blah, but often treats them as if they are a bunch of monkeys. To compound the problem, some managers manoeuvre themselves into positions of influence and try to impress by acting tough and talking hard, especially when it comes to removing their fellow colleagues for whatever reason appears to benefit the company. The human resource department is often seen as the Gestapo, always ruling in favour of the company. This adds to the problem faced by HR managers, many of whom are not enjoying the recognition they deserve. To complicate the situation, there are HR managers who hoard and guard information from those above them and below them. If this prevails, HR departments will continue to lose credibility. Re-engineering can be the saving grace for the HR profession.

The Industrial Revolution was based on the premise that brains are not required of machine operators. The revolution culminated in the development of the assembly line. Management scientists of old, such as

Frederick Taylor and the like, only served to reinforce the idea that even apes can be made to work at assembly lines. Industrial engineers and those who believe in the almighty hierarchy can be relied upon to direct the worker right to the very last detail, leaving absolutely nothing to individual initiative; and if some of this work can be automated, or computerized, then to hell with the people! This is, of course, not the attitude of most re-engineering experts, but their work appears to lead in that direction. The assumption is that re-engineering is done for one reason only and that is process redesign. If this assumption is carried to its furthest, the ideal company would be staffed by nothing but robots. Most self-styled re-engineering gurus have done nothing to contradict these assumptions. Robots work productively; people will always cause problems.

Re-engineering has entered the business world more or less on the industrial engineering side of the management science conflict. Carried to its extreme, it can be made to define every motion of the work to be done. Re-engineering is certainly capable of setting up a very detailed work process, completely ignoring the abilities of people, as well as totally eliminating any vestige of ingenuity on their part.

Identifying personnel problems

A full range of personnel problems can arise from a re-engineering project. Companies must realize that recruitment, training and retraining, job evaluation and re-evaluation, job grading and regrading, transfer, rotation, redeployment and outplacement may be needed.

The importance of people to the success of a re-engineering project makes this an area that should receive attention from day one. Three years after Dr Michael Hammer's book hit the stores, he pointed out a flaw. The *Wall Street Journal* reported that Hammer and other leaders of the re-engineering industry had forgotten about people. 'I wasn't smart enough about that,' Hammer was reported saying. 'I was reflecting my background and was insufficiently appreciative of the human dimension. I've learned that's critical.'

HR's participation can help identify problems while there is time to solve them without delaying the project, and can provide information concerning the strengths and weaknesses of each individual. It is also highly desirable for the new processes to be compatible with corporate personnel policies.

The problems that a re-engineering exercise will face may not surface until new processes have been designed. At that time, there is an immediate need to translate the skills of the current staff to the new work requirements.

When the re-engineering project begins to tackle staffing problems, the value of human capital will take on a new meaning. The key to a successful re-engineering effort is the workforce. The employees must have a sense of ownership so that the new operation will work; no redesign can be implemented if they fight it.

The problems that a re-engineering project must address to staff a new process can be intimidating. The result must be the right people, with the right skills, doing the newly defined work. Re-engineering must also deliver any necessary streamlining of the staff, and this will entail cutbacks.

During all this, the morale of the workforce should be kept at a high level. These tasks seem almost overwhelming, and many change projects have indeed been overwhelmed by them.

Fortunately, there are ways of solving the staff problems and managing the implementation of re-engineering projects that turn the difficulties in dealing with people into advantages. Of course workers may not be able to carry out functions as well as machines, but they can do some of their own implementation work. After all, shopfloor people know the shopfloor best. They can carry some of the burden of their own management, and can design and implement the new processes. In doing so, they solve their own morale and motivation problems. It is even possible for the workforce to exceed the design requirements specified by the re-engineering project. That is what makes human capital the most valuable resource.

Any process that increases its efficiency should achieve either higher output with the existing staff or the same output with fewer staff. Out of this will come issues like difficulty in retaining the right staff, loss of trust in management, high outplacement costs, adverse impact on productivity, and a definite tendency of the affected areas of the company toward restaffing themselves.

Re-engineering efforts will have produced a new set of processes, which will require staffing changes. New positions devoted to newly defined work will be created. These new jobs may be defined to approximate the old job descriptions, or may be designed *de novo*.

Job descriptions as we know them are not intended to tell anyone how to do work, which is one of the reasons they are of so little use as input to re-engineering. Re-engineering can help create more effective job descriptions by providing a clear explanation of the work, the work's relationship to the business and quantitative standards for performance.

RMM revisited

During re-engineering, retraining can be used as an alternative to sacking one employee and hiring another. The re-engineering process supports training design by providing detailed work process requirements: the specific background and skills of each position are related to the activities of the new process.

The widespread practice of using a rigid job-grading system to control compensation often results in a problem known as grade creep. This is due to pressure put on the system by managers seeking to reward their best performers. Theoretically, performance should not be the motivation for increasing grades. Grade creeps corrupt a business job-grading system and affect re-engineering because employee reassignments become difficult due to skewed grades. Management can take advantage of re-engineering to change the entire compensation policy.

Where give high performance awards to comp for low pay / better staff?

It is often said that nobody ever made a cent from morale. However, it is easy enough to lose big money from the lack of it. Companies that do not value the attitudes of their workforce do not value quality. Staff morale must be managed during a re-engineering project. This can be done by active and frequent communication on the project's status.

Also, to complement and support a continuing re-engineering process, a new HR management capability will be needed. Management must provide the funds and furnish the necessary support to ensure that.

It is important to be conscious of the fact that companies don't re-engineer processes; people do.

Re-engineering roles

How companies select and organize the people who actually do the re-engineering is critical to the success of the endeavour.

Hammer and Champy have seen the following roles emerge, either distinctly or in various combinations, during their work with companies that are re-engineering:

- leader – a senior executive who authorizes and motivates the re-engineering effort

- process owner – a manager with responsibility for a specific process and the re-engineering effort focused on it

- re-engineering team – a group of individuals dedicated to the re-engineering of a particular process, who diagnose existing process and oversee its redesign and implementation

- steering committee – a policy-making body of senior managers who develop the organization's overall re-engineering strategy and monitor its progress

- re-engineering tsar – an individual responsible for

developing re-engineering techniques and tools within the company and for achieving synergy across the company's separate re-engineering projects.

In an ideal world, the relationship among these is as follows. The *leader* appoints a *process owner*, who convenes a *re-engineering team* to re-engineer a process, with the assistance from the *tsar* and under the auspices of the *steering committee*.

These are the competences of a creative and fruitful re-engineer:

◆ sensitive – diplomatic, non-abrasive

◆ excellent communicator – able to solicit buy-in and ownership

◆ able to see the big picture – the trees from the forest

◆ accomplished achiever – good track record

◆ visionary – a futurist

◆ committed – have the stickability to see projects to fruition

◆ a leader – sets the pace, determines the tone

◆ creative – able to formulate outstanding alternatives

◆ credible – already enjoys liking and respect

◆ open – receptive to the ideas of others.

If you decide to use a consultant, you should be sure that you stay in the area of using the consultant effectively, rather than relying so heavily on the consultant that you lose control of the project and fail to develop the level of understanding that a closer involvement would have brought. You need to retain control of the activities in your own organization.

The role of the consultant

The first decision you must make is how you will use a consultant. Consultants can fill a variety of roles. Since you are the client, you should be able to choose the role and select a consultant based on his or her ability to fulfil it. If you go into the selection process with no particular role in mind, the chances are that the consultant will make that decision for you. While this is not necessarily bad, most clients prefer more control.

Reference

One way of using the consultant is as a living reference book, whose information will be transferred to you and your people during question-and-answer sessions and mini-lectures.

Catalyst

A broader use of the consultant would be for him or her to help you begin the project 'on the right foot', whether in the decision-making phase or after you have made the decision. At this early stage in the project, the presence of a third party can provide some comfort, as well as guidance, both to you and to your people.

Challenger

Another valuable role of the consultant is as an official 'devil's advocate' to challenge the assumptions on which you are operating, the decisions that you make regarding change, and the data that you collect – in short, to cause you to review all your past and current thinking about how things work both inside and outside the organization.

Outside eyes

In general, if the role of a consultant could be summed up, it would probably be described as a pair of outside eyes that can look at the organization as no one inside it can. A consultant coming into an organization for the first time sees conditions with which those inside have grown so accustomed that they no longer notice them. This ability to bring a fresh outlook to your organization is one of the chief advantages of using a consultant.

Time saver

The consultant's previous experience with re-engineering may help you bring the new organization up to speed more quickly. An experienced observer can spot any potential pitfalls and steer you safely away from them.

Monitor

A consultant may also serve to keep the re-engineering project on track. Re-engineering and its end results will become the consultant's chief interest in your organization. This means that he or she will continue to pull your attention back to the long-range re-engineering project when your operational crises threaten to distract you too much. When the alligators of day-to-day operations start nipping at your heels, the consultant will remind you that you need to be working on draining the swamp or those alligators will never go away. While consultants are sometimes criticized for their single-mindedness or narrow views, it is precisely this concentration that makes them valuable in keeping you on track.

Project manager

Sometimes, as in any project, it becomes tempting to use the consultant as a project manager. While the project ultimately may be very successful when handled this way, such arm's-length involvement on your part does not demonstrate commitment either to the process or to the final results.

Contracts with consultants come in two forms: those that agree to methods and amount of payment and those that specify the consultant's role. The former tend to be more formal and written. The latter are usually less formal, often unwritten, and frequently overlooked. Whether or not your organization and the consultant require the formally executed document, you must clarify the consultant's role and what you expect in terms of consulting services. Remember that most consulting watchdog bodies consider payment-for-performance arrangements unethical.

Developing a contract

During the past few years the income of many large management consulting firms has slipped, resulting in a number of layoffs. Furthermore, graduating MBAs are no longer seeking employment with large consulting firms, since that kind of career future looks doubtful. What has gone wrong?

First, let's go to the USA where Connie Irwin of William Dunk Partners (a survey company) conducted a poll among CEOs of 30 large American firms in order to discover their attitudes towards the quality of work performed by the management consulting firms they had retained. Their responses were along the following lines:

◆ Clients pay too much money to teach consultants the business.

◆ Senior consultants are excellent marketing people when it comes to their firms' expertise, but once the assignment is contracted for, the client never sees those senior people again. Instead, the project is turned over to 'green peas' (neophytes).

The clients were then asked to rate the 'big six'. None received an 'excellent' rating. The top one, McKinsey, only rated 'above average'.

There are approximately 150 000 independent consultants in the USA alone. They cover 310 fields of expertise. If we expand our view to cover the entire advice business by including psychiatry, accounting, law and health-care counselling, we find a population of 450 000. Unlike medical doctors, consultants without work will, like lawyers, create havoc. Doctors can't create disease.

In Singapore, the profession has been burgeoning exponentially too. The last two years have witnessed a proliferation of consultants who claim to specialize in helping companies become ISO-certified. There are said to be some 50 different master's degree programmes offered by all kinds of organizations – from the Singapore Productivity and Standards Board to the Singapore Institute of Management to excellent, credible private centres of learning like the Asia Pacific Management Centre to the mom-and-pop operators who work from a hole-in-the-wall at department stores.

One shudders at the thought of the qualifications of the so-called 'consultants' teaching those programmes.

Anyone can call himself a consultant. Even consultants I hire joke about it: anyone who is unemployed, possesses a briefcase and can talk and chew gum at the same time can be a consultant. I have heard of someone who used to be a cigarette salesman, has never been to school and now calls himself vice-president of a consulting firm! There are consultants who list qualifications from McDonald's or Holiday Inn University in their CVs. There are those who are like the after-dinner speakers of old – the same old subject but over 50 different titles. Then there are those who write books about how to be achievers but whose personal lives are far from exemplary – they engage in backbiting, slander and libel.

The trouble is, as I've mentioned before, if an axe is all you have, you'll see every problem as a tree. Consultants will only sell you what they know. Someone who proclaims him or herself a specialist in decision making and creative thinking will tend to think that every organizational ill can be solved by a few days of training on decision making and creative thinking! A consultant who only knows job analysis and evaluation will think that what every organization needs is to have their employees' jobs analysed and evaluated. Similarly someone who specializes in 'airy-fairy' subjects like 'unleashing one's hidden power' will think that all a company needs is to send its employees to some motivational training session.

Users of consulting services must be discerning. A recent *Fortune* article on consulting was entitled 'In search of suckers – a growing army of Tom Peters' wannabes are making millions peddling advice . . .'.

Consultants' competency levels

In any given profession – law, medicine, dentistry, accounting and consulting – the competency levels break down in the same manner:

1   The top 20 per cent are a credit to their professions. They are experts in what they do and they practise this expertise in an efficient, innovative, dedicated, thoroughly professional and ethical manner. They are mature and are able to prevent themselves from being manipulated by members of their own organization or someone from the client organization. (Consulting, unfortunately, like modelling and advertising, is a bitchy business.) They are also culturally sensitive, sharp in dealing with clients and do not become henchmen of the 'top client'. (In Singapore there is a senior manager from Europe who has gained a reputation for himself among the consulting profession as someone who treats consultants from various firms as hired guns.) These honourable consultants are usually specialists, not all things to all men. I was told of a consultant who went to Australia on donated funds to study to be a social worker but 'something happened' along the way

and he returns as a business adviser and seminar speaker – he may be versatile but he has no known expertise unless you consider gift of the gab as an expertise.

The success rate of sterling consultants like those mentioned earlier is over 95 per cent and they more than earn their fees.

2   The next 30 per cent are adequate to their tasks, but never innovative in their approach. They are rarely dedicated, but rather consider their occupations a 'good way to earn a living'. Their success rate is 50 to 70 per cent. I know one person who has never been a consultant in his life and he managed to negotiate a starting gross monthly salary of almost S$10 000. Certainly a good way to earn a living.

3   The bottom 50 per cent are the ones who give their respective professions a bad name and dreadful publicity. It is they who have succeeded in creating the adversarial environment in the advice business, i.e. doctor versus patient, lawyer versus client, consultant versus client. The jokes about doctors, lawyers and consultants are legion. Indeed, as many hurt their clients or patients as help them.

I am extremely critical because I think this is one profession that cannot afford not to be credible.

How to identify the top 20 per cent of the consulting profession?

Qualifications

The background of consultants is that they usually have a professional qualification or a business degree on top of their first one. They will commonly have at least five years' managerial experience, that is, they will have run a department or division in a company. They will also often have worked overseas. It is still rare for first-degree graduates to enter the profession as soon as they leave the university.

What consultancies look for primarily when recruiting is high intelligence plus some particular expertise. What counts much more is a good first degree plus good business training, so that an MBA is almost a passport to the profession. The local office of an international consulting firm has nine consultants, three of whom are PhDs and the rest MBAs; all have held senior management positions in various parts of the world – that's consulting power for you! The brochure of a consulting firm in the UK states that of their 121 consultants 69 have masters or PhD degrees or their professional equivalents. Average age of the consultants is 46. Almost all had progressed through at least two management jobs before becoming consultants – facts which would make any client feel comfortable.

McKinsey combs through more than 50 000 résumés a year just to hire about 550 new consultants – a stringent process. The firm is only keen on those who have studied at Harvard, Wharton, Northwestern or Stanford. One in five associates becomes a principal, or junior partner, in the first six years. Only half of those who become principals end up as directors but they are well rewarded. Directors can earn as much as US$2 million a year in salary and bonus, and all partners receive equity in the firm. No Mickey Mouse stuff here! No 35-year-old kids as partners here! McKinsey believes that gone are the days when consulting was still known as 'management engineering' and everyone was called a 'principal consultant' or 'chief analyst'. You have to work for it!

Hiring practices

A friend of mine once almost used a consulting firm which employs no one, using only freelancers to do their work. No E or CPF (employee or central provident fund) payment as mandated by the law in Malaysia and Singapore is paid and the independent contractors are not covered by insurance and do not enjoy any basic employee benefits. When there is no work, there is no pay as these freelancers are then 'put on the beach'. The firm has a good product but what you have here is a motley group of demotivated, disgruntled rejects teaching you how to run your business and charging you for it. Being willing to work under such terms, these individuals are also probably of questionable background.

Do you want them as your consultants? I have also known of husband-and-wife consulting teams – the wife works for one consulting company and the husband for another. That gives some people an uneasy feeling.

Selling approaches

There is no such thing as a free lunch. If a consultancy offers to conduct a 'free' analysis of your operations or offers to conduct a preliminary study of your business at their own expense, look out. I will bet my last cent there is a catch there somewhere.

Benefits versus costs

The relationship between costs and benefits is an important factor in deciding on the use of a consultant. In principle, this use is justified only if the benefits are higher than the costs.

Contingency fees – fees determined as a proportion of savings achieved by the client thanks to the consultants – have been banned as unprofessional by many consultants' associations and individual firms.

As a matter of fact, be wary of consultants who promise savings, especially which they themselves will purportedly 'measure' for you. Any attempt to evaluate results should be independent and undertaken by the client's external auditor.

Savings very often force consultants to 'achieve' and 'demonstrate measurable results' in the short term, which can often be done relatively easily to the detriment of longer-term interests of the client. A couple of years ago several banks in the Singapore region had to rehire staff who were laid off. These disillusioned employees were initially axed because the banks' consultants were keen to show savings by 'POPs' – taking People Off the Payrolls.

In cases where consultants engineer 'savings base agreements' with their clients, clients must ensure that the methods used do not unfairly favour the consultants. The problem is that some consultants are so good at that game clients are befuddled. So do make use of your own 'bean counters' when it comes to such situations.

Consulting approach

There is an extremely wide range of consulting approaches, but a typical one is: entry, diagnosis, action planning, implementation and termination.

Too many consultancies follow an off-the-shelf approach designed to sell you a big project. Any consultant worth his or her salt will be willing to agree to your requirements. Demand that throughout the diagnosis and implementation stage you reserve the right to exercise ultimate control of the consulting process. At termination stage, ensure that the good results can perpetuate. If a consultant claims to provide follow-up for a specified period after the project, insist on speaking with executives of a company which is still receiving such follow-up.

Third-party testimonials

Consultants like to flash reference letters around but you must telephone the writers of these letters to check their authenticity and to ensure that these references are still current. True, some companies do not wish to make it public knowledge that they use consultants but most consulting firms ought to be able to provide you with a client list. Talk to the people on the client list, arrange to visit them and listen to what they say about their experience with the consultants you are considering using. Generally the longer the consulting firm has been around, the longer the client list.

Affiliations

Although I can accept it, some purists persist that consulting services offered by accounting/auditing firms should not be used. 'It is unethical,' they say, 'these people have access to highly confidential financial information and you run the risk of being raided [taken over].'

In a number of countries management consultants have established voluntary professional associations to represent their interests and regulate the activities of both individual consultants and consulting firms. Professional associations of management consultants attach great importance to the codes of professional conduct (ethics, professional practice) which they use as instruments to establish the profession and protect its integrity and to inform clients about behavioural rules observed by the consultants.

There are also attempts at certifying consultants. For example, in 1980 the Institute of Management Consultants in the UK established written entrance examinations.

Webster's Dictionary defines certify as 'to attest as being true or as representing or as meeting a standard'. The National Bureau of Professional Management Consultants, USA, has established standards for the certification of its members who have over ten years of consulting experience. The bureau is an independent organization established to give recognition to consultants by registering them through a national certification programme.

Finally, a word about what consulting is not. There is an abundance of case histories of successful projects carried out by some consultants in order to rescue companies facing trouble. They have created an image of consultants as knights in shining armour, galloping at full speed to right wrongs. It also implies that consultants can resolve virtually any problem. That is unrealistic. Consultants do not provide miracle solutions.

In the end, consultants are like any other business people; the professional ones won't lie, cheat or coerce. If you've been wise in selecting and using them, they can deliver a return to your bottom line that's ten times what you laid out in cash. If you don't do your homework, however, expect to be taken for a long, unpleasant ride. One that you'll deserve.

Chapter 11
Redesign – Aiming for the Jugular

With all the groundwork done, it is now time to redesign.

For a writer, staring at a blank computer monitor can be a frightening prospect! For a re-engineer, the first redesign session poses a similar challenge. At this session you have to invent a new way for your organization to do work.

Of course it is not as simple as that. Redesign is the most nakedly creative part of the entire re-engineering process. More than any other, it demands imagination and, according to Hammer and Champy, even a touch of craziness. In redesigning processes you have to abandon the familiar and seek the outrageous. Redesign requires you to suspend your belief in the rules, procedures and values that you've honoured your whole working lives. This is the time when sacred cows are slaughtered and paradigms are shifted. Redesign is unnerving precisely because you are anointed to do whatever it takes.

Shigeo Shingo, one of the developers of the Just-In-Time production system that helped make Toyota the most productive automobile manufacturer in the world, once said that the slogan 'Eliminate waste' ought to be changed to 'Find waste'. Shingo believes that if you really want to make improvements, never accept the *status quo* – search for problems where you think none exists. 'If it ain't broke, keep looking.'

There is no textbook formula for redesigning work processes. From past experiences, the following thoughts, issues and themes recur:

1   Work is best organized around outcomes (for example, a processed claim) rather than tasks (verifying claim information), thus enabling people to measure the direct impact of their work on the organization. This, in turn, provides management with the means to hold individuals and teams accountable. Work designed around outcomes means processes are grouped together to eliminate the need for too many different people handling them, resulting in excessive checking and cross-checking. When work is organized around outcomes, jobs become vertically loaded, meaning that people can act on information that they generate themselves. Such compression of work significantly reduces cycle times and improves responsiveness.

2   As few people as possible should be involved in the performance of a process. Usually workers spend time checking on each other. This is because natural processes have been fragmented and people are hired to put the pieces together again. In a re-engineered environment, the rank and file is empowered and equipped with skills and resources for multi-tasking. Most organizations contain at least one extra level of

hierarchy. Its existence serves to assure management that all important functions will be performed.

3   You don't always need to be an expert to redesign a process. As long as there is input of work, which is done, resulting in an output, you have a process in existence. Any process can be redesigned for greater effectiveness. Viewing a process with a new set of eyes helps.

4   Being an outsider helps. There are times when I deliberately refuse to assign a consultant to another project of a similar nature. When a person arrives on the scene 'cold' he or she does so without preconceived notions and hangups. This person comes with fresh ideas, is not part of the problem and is more clear-headed.

5   You have to discard preconceived notions. You may detect similarities in the causes of certain organizational dysfunction but you cannot assume that because factor X was the cause of plant failure in company A, the same factor X is also the culprit in company B.

6   It's important to see through the (internal and external) customer's eyes. All that talk about customer service is useless unless processes are re-engineered to enable workers to provide direct access to customers or to enhance that capability. This allows for timely accurate responses to customer needs.

7   Redesign is best done in teams. Two heads are better than one. Team members can 'piggy-ride' on each others' ideas.

8 You don't need to know much about the current process. There is no need to beat a dead horse to death – remember you need not know the minutest of details, otherwise you'll suffer from 'analysis paralysis'.

9 It's not hard to have great ideas. You need to put creative thinking techniques into practice (see Chapter 9).

10 It can be fun. So is there fun in dangerous driving. Therefore, while re-engineering, remember the human side of enterprise. Will people be hurt? Is it an excuse to fire people? Are you giving people enough clout and tools to work effectively?

Recurring themes in re-engineered organizations

1 Several jobs are combined into one. Work which is fragmented needs to be put together again.

2 Workers make decisions by acquiring information they need. Access to accurate information and a clear understanding of policies and practices empowers people to make informed, competent decisions. No longer bound by cumbersome approval processes and outmoded bureaucracies, workers can react quickly and respond to customer needs as they arise.

3 The steps in the process are performed in a natural order. There is no need to revisit steps and procedures.

4 Processes have multiple versions. This is the flexibility which re-engineering can offer.

5 Work is performed when and where it makes the

most sense, either in-house or subcontracted out. Procedures are not followed simply because 'we've always done it this way'.

6   Checks and controls are reduced. Some American banks have empowered customer representatives to approve loan requests within one hour over the telephone. In a traditional environment the normal process takes at least four weeks. How can this happen? It is possible once people have access to the type of information they need for decision making.

7   Excessive checking is minimized. In a re-engineered environment, the organization has been transformed and the degree of openness and maturity allows people to act with integrity.

8   Work units change, from functional departments to process teams. The Kuala Lumpur Stock Exchange is an example of a progressive organization where work is done by self-managed work teams. In the US automobile industry, it used to require at least five years to take a vehicle from concept to showroom. Each work unit, such as design, engineering, manufacturing, assembly, marketing and sales, functioned independently and in sequence. A vehicle concept required approval before it went to engineering, and manufacturing was not consulted until all the engineering work was complete. (Ever wondered why you have all those people sitting around, doing nothing?) This over-the-wall approach not only took time, it also created complexities and problems that increased the final cost of the vehicle. In the re-engineered environment, both

cycle time and cost of manufacturing are significantly reduced.

9 Jobs change, from simple tasks to multidimensional work. Workers are motivated by the enrichment that job enlargement brings about. When people can communicate cross-functionally and cross-organizationally, then work can be performed simultaneously instead of linearly.

10 People's roles change, from controlled to empowered. Encouraged, workers develop their ability and willingness to make significant decisions.

11 Job preparation changes, from training to education. The approach now is more holistic. You don't just teach and train, you educate. The difference is that workers are fully aware of the total picture not just parts of a puzzle. The maxim 'They practise mushroom management here – they keep me in the dark and feed me bulls***' no longer holds true.

12 Focus of performance measures and compensation shifts from activity to results. It is results that count and not how many subordinates you have. Hammer and Champy say that traditional Hay point schemes, in which the size of a person's salary is a function of the number of subordinates that a person has working for him or her and the size of that person's budget, don't fit into a process-oriented environment.

13 Achievement criteria change, from performance to ability. Harry Pearce, General Motors' executive vice-president, recently said that GM's

old compensation system was such that 'If you want to just hand out gratuities to people you like, that's the way you'd set it up.' After re-engineering, employees are not rewarded for what they know or claim to know but for what they actually do for the organization. Paul Allaire, CEO of Xerox, said 'If you talk about change and then leave the reward and recognition system exactly the same, nothing changes.'

14 Values change, from protective to productive. Nobody is defensive, everybody chips in. There is comradeship and camaraderie.

15 Managers change, from supervisors to coaches. There is no longer a need to breathe down people's necks. Managers need to orchestrate. A manager shifts from supervisor to coach, from boss to facilitator, and from tactician to strategist. The manager is no longer someone who cracks the whip. He is now a futurist, a planner, an obstacle remover, a subject matter expert, a process facilitator, a technical adviser and an interteam co-ordinator.

16 Organizational structures change, from hierarchical to flat. The outcome of a re-engineered organization is that you often end up with a flatter one.

17 Executives change, from scorekeepers to leaders. Of course the bottom line counts, but under pressure to keep scores most members of senior management forget their leadership roles. With an organization in good health, executives can concentrate on being leaders.

Chapter 12
Information Technology as an Enabler

Re-engineer first, then put in the information technology (IT). Not the other way round. You don't put the cart before the horse. Why cement cowpaths? Why simply lay technology over a cumbersome, inefficient process full of non-value-added steps?

Many companies continue to computerize obsolete processes. Part of the reason is a general lack of understanding of what IT can do.

To begin with, introducing new technologies is itself not an answer to most business problems. Only after the problem domain has been carefully studied can an appropriate technology be selected and applied. The Edison story is a classic example of the misapplication of technology. Thomas Edison proposed a technology for mechanizing the voting procedures for the US Congress. Using his technology, each congressman would have a panel (labelled 'Yea' and 'Nay') and would press the appropriate button whenever a bill was put to a vote. The vote could then be tallied in seconds rather than the hours it normally took to manually count slips of paper with each vote. The results proved disastrous: though the machines worked just as Edison had promised, they did not address the root causes of the apparent problem. The time it took to count the votes was actually a necessary part of the process. That time was devoted to negotiating and debating. Edison's mechanization solved a problem that did not exist, and his proposal was thrown out. So instead of encompassing the entire range of new technologies that could enable business processes, this chapter will describe four technologies that enable re-engineering itself. These four technologies – distributed computing platforms, client-server architectures, workflow software, and application development tools – together facilitate the creation of new designs and enable the iterative development of those designs. (I am indebted to Daniel Petrozzo of International Data Operations and John Stepper of Morgan Stanley whose authoritative knowledge of IT has contributed much to my own understanding.)

Distributed computing platforms

Increasing business needs have culminated in the monolithic computers of the mainframe era. But mainframes are expensive and buying or leasing a multi-million dollar machine means a long-term commitment to a single vendor. Many organizations have shifted away from centralized computing toward distributed computing. A distributed computing system is defined as 'one in which multiple autonomous processors, possibly of different kinds, are interconnected by a communication subnet to interact in a co-operative way to achieve an overall goal'. Instead of a gigantic mainframe to support all of a business's information processing, the information system comprises a number of computers connected by a network and running special software so that the work of the processors can be co-ordinated. Price is certainly an attraction, resulting in smaller computers exhibiting a more superior price/performance ratio. Combined with fibre networks and distributed messaging software, distributed sets of small machines are attractive alternatives to mainframes. Also, distributed systems have a single system image (appear as one system to any user), achieve better performance and provide higher reliability, all for less money than a single processor system.

Yet another advantage is that distributed systems have higher fault tolerance. This means if a processor fails or if the network between some processors fails, the system still can function in some meaningful way. For example, if there's a hardware failure somewhere, the software is intelligent enough to recognize a failure state and switch to the use of reserve components, masking the failure from the rest of the system. Masking a failure means that the system continues to provide the standard specified service despite a component failure.

Finally, distributed systems are flexible because processors can be added as additional capacity is needed. What's more, these processors do not all have to be the same. Different types of processors can communicate because interface standards have been established, and each vendor adheres to the standards.

Distributed platforms enable the re-engineering of processes by facilitating data sharing and iterative development. With software that allows users to communicate across systems and maintain a single system image, the company can gradually eliminate data redundancy, remove the need for a synchronization mechanism and, more important, eliminate the problems that arise from inconsistencies between the different copies of the data.

Further, the combination of low cost and flexibility of distributed platforms means that anyone who re-engineers can begin implementing an information system to support new designs without having to know exactly what the new system will do eventually. Just after the initial re-engineering of a process, you are unlikely to know how many people will use the system or what type of database queries they will need to perform; so you could not possibly know what type of hardware and software you will need to support the complete design. Thus, distributed platforms lend themselves to an iterative development approach and let you minimize the risk associated with buying or leasing expensive equipment or making premature system design decisions.

In the past, building software was like giving instructions to someone on how to build a space shuttle. You write down all of the instructions in sequence and include logic or directions for the handling of special cases. ('If part 5.2 is not loose, go to step 6; if it has been tightened, go to section 22.2 for instructions on validating screw tightness,' etc.) As programs became larger and more complex, the logic became more and more enmeshed. The result would be what programmers refer to as 'spaghetti code'. How to untangle the spaghetti? Programmers create modules of software which perform specific functions and then link them together to form a single application.

Client-server architectures

Client-server architectures advance this concept further still. They divide programs into two general categories – a *client* initiating requests for resources and a *server* receiving the requests – performing the functions and returning the result.

Client-server architectures will facilitate the evolutionary development of an information system supporting your new business design. As you iteratively implement new design ideas, you can create or redesign clients and servers without having to change the rest of the system. This is because clients do not know how servers are carrying out their functions. The only thing that clients know about servers is how to request their resource. In general, the physical implementation of individual clients and servers is abstracted from the rest of the system. Thus, a database server may be rewritten to interface with a new database management system, but the rest of the system is unaffected as long as the means of requesting the resource remains the same.

Workflow software

One common cause of process problems is that system functions are not tied to the tasks in a process. This causes several consequences. Because there are no corresponding changes to the supporting information systems while changes to the process are being made, manual reconciliation and laborious checks become necessary. No automated tracking is possible and this can affect customer service. For example, if the system cannot tell precisely when service personnel are expected to sign off a job, other customers waiting for service will only receive vague 'our people will probably be there end of the week' type promises.

Workflow software not only allows a user to define a process on-line, it can also include information on dependencies between tasks. It is thus useful for work assignment and routing, scheduling, work list management, and automatic status and process metrics. By using such software and providing all people involved in the process with access to the system hosting that software, companies can enable a new process design or even achieve significant improvements in their existing processes.

Application development tools facilitate iterative development of a new design by enabling programmers to rapidly develop and deploy system functions to users. This is a far cry from the days when programmers had no easy way to specify what a computer should do and how it should do it. They had to specify the exact sequence of zeros and ones code that the computer would process! Today application development tools have greatly improved programmer productivity.

Application development tools

If IT's potential for business change is to be achieved, it must be viewed as an enabler of process innovation. Thomas Davenport, business professor at the University of Texas in Austin, has said that opportunities for supporting process innovation with IT fall into at least nine different categories.

◆ Automational – eliminating excessive human labour from a process

◆ Informational – capturing process information for purposes of understanding

◆ Sequential – changing process sequence, or enabling parallelism

◆ Tracking – closely monitoring process status and objects

◆ Analytical – improving analysis of information and decision making

◆ Geographical – co-ordinating processes across distances

◆ Integrative – co-ordinating between tasks and processes

◆ Intellectual – capturing and distributing intellectual assets

◆ Disintermediating – eliminating intermediaries from a process

Information technology can have important implication for key business processes. But technology itself cannot perform miracles. Some people mistakenly believe that implementing state-of-the-art technology alone with the biggest and the fastest machines will improve an organization's effectiveness and solve its problems. Nothing could be further from the truth. Innovations in the harnessing of technology must be combined with a sensitivity to human considerations.

Part IV
STEP FOUR

Sustaining Long-Term Results

Chapter 13
Perpetuation – Now and
Forever More

Now that the organization has been redesigned, how do you support and sustain the rebirth?

A powerful way of achieving buy-in and ownership is through effective and continuous involvement, deployment and utilization of people. Many re-engineered organizations have people working in numerous self-directed work teams. For increased flexibility, avoid any situation that encourages rigidity in the face of changing business conditions. Members of high-performance teams can become so accustomed to working together that they begin to think alike and to see the world from similar perspectives. This homogeneity can eventually make them reluctant to accept changes in the way that they operate. They succumb to groupthink. They may become complacent, which can lead them to abandon their quest for improvement, or they may remain a high-performance team but no longer do what you want them to do. Rowing well in the wrong direction is worse than not rowing at all.

There must be some degree of flexibility in the composition of teams. It can be encouraged through rotation of individuals from one team to another. Some organizations place so much emphasis on rotation that teams are structured to be of similar sizes

Rotation of team members

and to involve the same length of time for learning skills, so that rotation between them can be formal and planned. At specified intervals, a certain percentage of the organization's population rotates to different teams.

Rotation need not be too formal nor should optimal structure be sacrificed to gain more flexibility or mobility between teams. People should be allowed and encouraged to move to other teams on a relatively regular basis. This belief is rooted in several concerns.

There often exist within organizations conflicts that euphemistically are referred to as personality clashes, although fortunately they are usually rare. Sometimes clashes tend to follow the same people from one spot to another in the organization. When this is the case, the problem may lie with the individual and cannot be solved by a move to another team. These situations are difficult to confront, but they must be handled so that the rest of the organization can continue its business between pairs of individuals who are good performers with a history of high performance in other situations. Moving one or both of the warring individuals will often solve the problem; frequently they will seek the moves themselves.

Movement between teams is also important to prevent them from stagnating. When the same people work together over the years, performing virtually the same function, they often cease to look for ways to improve. They become satisfied with their relationships, their roles and their activities. Often it takes an outsider, someone new to the team, to stir things up, ask questions, and propose new ways to improve results. In this instance a little conflict is not entirely negative.

When you are looking for constant improvement, you must create an environment that nurtures such improvement. Static teams do not provide that environment. For this reason, it is not enough merely to allow people to move to other positions on other teams; they must be encouraged to make such moves.

Some organizations have done this by building assignments on multiple teams into a skill-based pay system. In other words, in any given team there are only so many skills to acquire; to be of more value to the organizations – and hence to increase their pay – workers must have skills on several teams.

A more subtle approach is used currently for management personnel in many organizations, whereby to be considered for higher positions within management an individual must have experience in a broad range of products or services, as well as several different functions. The motivation to move then becomes the opportunity for promotion.

Re-engineering steering committee

As more and more people are involved in re-engineering your organization, a sense of ownership will intensify. This can only augur well for your organization.

The re-engineering steering committee is an optional aspect of the re-engineering governance structure. Some companies swear by it, others live without it, and others swear at it. The steering committee is a collection of senior managers, usually including but not limited to the process owners, who plan the organization's overall re-engineering strategy. The leaders should chair this group.

Far-ranging issues that transcend the scope of individual processes and projects are aired in the steering committee. This group decides, for example, how resources should be allocated. Process owners and their teams come to the steering committee for help when they run into problems that they can't resolve on their own. Part Supreme Court, part mutual aid society, part House of Lords, the steering committee can do much to help an extensive re-engineering programme succeed.

Resistance to change

Just as change is inevitable so is resistance to change. Paradoxically, organizations both promote and resist change. As an agent of change, the organization asks prospective customers or clients to change their current purchasing habits by switching to the company's product or service and asks current customers to change by increasing their purchases. At the same time, the organization resists change in that its structure and control systems protect the daily tasks of producing a product service from uncertainties in the environment.

A commonly held view is that all resistance to change needs to be overcome, but that is not always the case. Resistance to change can be compared to the property of materials that restricts the passage of electrical current and causes the material to give off heat, a property known as resistance. A frequently quoted example is that the heating coils in a toaster, waffle iron, and hairdryer all use this principle. If the resistance is complete, however, no current flows and thus no heat is given off. Resistance to the passage of current is useful as long as some current can flow through the material.

Similarly, organizational resistance need not be eliminated entirely but can be managed and controlled for the benefit of the organization. By revealing a legitimate concern that a proposed change may not be good for the organization, resistance may alert the organization to investigate and re-examine the change.

These are the six basic organizational sources of resistance:

◆ Overheating – so many organizational endeavours are in place that it becomes unrealistic to expect employees' behaviour to be stable.

◆ Narrow focus of change – if the scope of change is too narrow, there will be problems. Most attempts at redesigning jobs are unsuccessful because the organization structure within which jobs must function is inappropriate.

◆ Group inertia – negative group norms in existence.

◆ Threatened expertise – job redesign may transfer the responsibility for a specialized task from the current expert to someone else, thus threatening the specialist's expertise and building his or her resistance to the change.

◆ Threatened power – redistribution of decision-making authority may threaten an individual's power relationship with others.

◆ Resource allocation – anyone satisfied with current resource allocation methods may resist any change he or she believes will threaten his/her future allocations.

Individual sources of resistance include habit, security, economic factors, fear of the unknown, lack of awareness and social factors.

Resistance and maintenance leading to perpetuation may be managed by education and communication, participation and involvement, facilitation and support, negotiation and agreement, manipulation and co-optation and, finally, coercion.

The widely known concept of UNFREEZING, CHANGING and REFREEZING in a change process is a refreshing albeit overused reminder of the dynamics of change. Figuratively speaking, you thaw out old, destructive behaviours, change them to positive behaviours and cast them in concrete.

A more relevant way of presenting the concept would be to look at change as a four-step process:

Four-step process of change management

1   Mechanical compliance – the process has been redesigned, but at this stage it is normal for compliance to be somewhat mechanical. This stage is sometimes referred to as the 'valley of despair'.

2   Comprehension and identification – after about 21 days of mechanical compliance, true understanding usually sets in, the process user 'sees the light' and fully understands the need for change in the first place. He or she climbs out of the 'valley' and begins to perform at an acceptable level.

3   Refinement and internalization – now the process user is able to refine and continuously improve the changed process to enhance its effectiveness.

4   Perpetuation – the results are maintained for good.

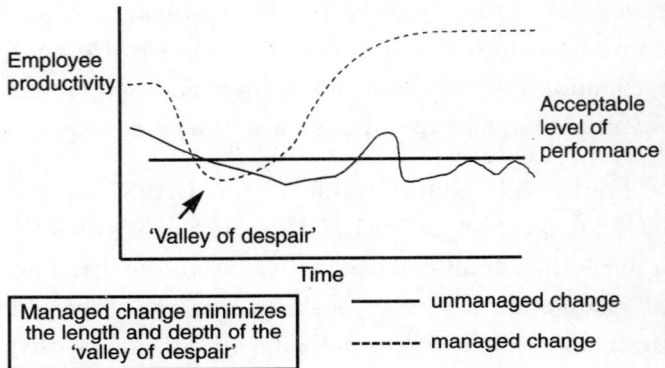

Figure 13.1 *The change curve*

Figure 13.1 illustrates the process.

Maintaining the change

Every organization, big or small, would like to change for the better. But can positive change be maintained? Consider the following demoralizing facts. Fact one: 85 per cent of Fortune 1000 companies have downsized workforces in the past five years, but their overhead rates remain significantly above the best global competitors. Fact two: hundreds of organizations in North America have undertaken large restructurings, but 52 per cent of executives surveyed say these efforts have not met original targets. Fact three: billions have been spent on automating inefficient business processes, but information systems or expensive hardware have proven to be among the least effective at improving productivity. Fact four: hundreds of leading corporations have made acquisitions to build synergies by integrating different departments, but only one in three investments has generated a return greater than the buyer's cost of capital.

Seven out of ten management initiatives fail, not because they are bad ideas, but because they are not properly implemented and – most importantly – sustained. The downsizers mentioned above failed because their main attention was on ridding themselves of people, not on changing the remaining staff's behaviour and business processes. The reformers failed because they concentrated on the organization's structure, not on people and what they do. The big spenders intent on improving efficiency failed because they concentrated on technology, not on the people applying it. And the would-be synergizers failed because they concentrated on integrating plants rather than people.

Change has to be managed. Change management is best defined as the process which focuses on exciting and enabling individuals and groups to take responsibility for realizing the vision of their organization and the development of their own potential.

One company that has managed change very well is Motorola. From its beginnings in 1928 producing car radios, to the latest in cellular telephones, Motorola has always been ahead in the rapidly advancing field of electronics. It now employs more than 100 000 people worldwide. Like many companies Motorola has shifted much of its production to other countries to take advantage of low operating costs. Mexico has been particularly appealing because of its cheap labour and its proximity to the USA. Motorola's Guadalajara plant, however, recently experienced some difficulties due to super inflation in the Mexican economy and low morale among employees.

Motorola management knew that traditional means of improving quality and productivity would not work because of the unique characteristics of the Mexican labour market, where the priorities are family, religion, and work – in that order. The most important element of the process was to recognize two key values in Mexican culture: teamwork and pride in accomplishment. The focus on competitiveness that worked so well in North America would clearly not be appropriate in the Guadalajara plant, so the organizational change model was adapted to suit the culture of the country.

Senior management introduced a seven-step change model for organization effectiveness in Mexico. They began by ensuring that all employees knew of Motorola's vision to be a world-class manufacturer. The other steps included the development of strategies consistent with that vision; changing organizational structures to fit with the strategies; matching staff to the organization's needs; training workers in essential skills; using a participative style; and developing systems to manage the company on a daily basis.

The programme was a success. Productivity has increased by 30 to 40 per cent plantwide, on-time deliveries are nearly 100 per cent, cycle times have been halved, and employee morale is high. These improvements came about because the change process had been managed well.

Part V

Looking Ahead

Chapter 14
What Next?

There are three approaches to predicting the future, the use of:

◆ projecting – the most conservative approach, using currently available information to arrive at imaginatively foreseeable implications for the future

◆ paradoxes – the unpredictable nature of the future requires us to take a different approach and things which at first glance seem paradoxical or even nonsensical, viewed from certain angles, will make perfect sense, and the future veers off in an unprecedented direction

◆ paradigms – the first two approaches are evolutionary whereas this is revolutionary, raising the question: what if a paradigm shift – a fundamental change in the nature of the game – occurs in the business world?

I do not want to be labelled a soothsayer. There are already too many of them among us. However, there are some questions which must be asked.

What will you be like 20 years from now? How old will you be? What challenges, concerns, passages does one experience at the age you will be those years?

Don't just read this through without reflection. Stop and ponder. How might the future affect you? What work will you be doing? What will you like? What will your industry or organization be encountering? What expectations will they have of you? As your own futurist, what do you believe is likely, probable or possible in the next 20 years?

Everything we think and do from this second on will affect only tomorrow. Yesterday is gone, and today exists for only a brief moment. We spend the remainder of our lives in tomorrows.

The prospect that tomorrow may hold a lot more change than the recent past can be very unsettling. If the future will be so different that no prediction can be expected to present even a reasonable picture, then how can any plans be made? How can any preparations be expected to give advantage? Is the safest course just to invest in gold and wait?

The answer is that, even with the pace of change increasing, the direction of future events is not completely unpredictable.

The end of the cold war has shown that economics and commerce will finally overwhelm force, ideology and politics. Nearer home, the courting of Myanmar by ASEAN (the Association of South East Asian Nations), despite the human rights atrocities committed by the country's military junta, is a case in point. Business makes strange bedfellows these days. Whatever high ideals remain in the world today seem to be subordinated to the universal drive to make money. Well, this actually gives humanity an opportunity that has never presented itself before. Perhaps from the current political and social climate, there can grow the first great global society.

The history of humankind suggests that *homo sapiens habilis* always invents tools to take the labour out of labour-intensive activities. McCormick reapers and, later, huge combine-harvesters have replaced millions of human harvesters of crops. Automated looms, assembly lines and robots have replaced manufacturing labour. When service and information work come to dominate employment and labour costs, the computer and re-engineering appear to automate and reduce this labour.

The *Wall Street Journal* (16 March 1993) asserts that re-engineering has the potential to wipe out 30 per cent of all jobs in the US economy.

Guesses about what comes next for human workers include:

◆ Entertainment – tens of thousands of computer channels and hundreds of millions of fibre optic pathways will create an ever-expanding need for 'infotainment' (entertainment–information) soft-ware to become 'downloadable' from the information superhighway. The question is whether the millennium of increased leisure time will ever arrive. Despite dishwashers, washing machines, thermal cookers, and the microwave and cars, computers and the cellular phone, the percentage of human time spent in work has steadily increased since the Middle Ages (although in the UK, work hours actually fell in the nineteenth and twentieth centuries until 1980, when they began to rise again). People now work about ten hours a week more than they did 40 years ago. It looks as if the only people able to enjoy the increase in entertainment will be an increasingly alienated underclass who can't afford it.

◆ Health care – another extension of an existing knowledge/service economy component. Whatever the prospects for health care reform, ever-advancing medical technology – 'virtual' surgical operations are now possible, and in the future devices the size of molecules may be injected into your bloodstream to correct your health problems – and an ageing population all but guarantees that health care's share of employment and economy will continue to grow.

◆ Biotechnology – genetic engineering advances

that will further revolutionize agriculture, medicine and even computers, based in molecular or biological transistors – artificial brain cells connected in neural nets – may well change the very definition of what life is.

◆ The environment – massive redeployment of human effort and resources to clean up and maintain planet earth.

◆ Entrepreneurship – the *laissez-faire* notion that people in a steadily growing economy will create employment in serving markets for as yet unthought of products and services.

◆ Science, art, literature and culture – a variant of the entertainment idea. What little discretionary time people may be left with will be spent on 'quality' pursuits such as self-development, discovery and creation – done in an entertaining manner. Already infotainment has made inroads into our living-rooms.

◆ Space – colonization of the moon and Mars. If this is achieved, manufacturing in space won't be too far-fetched an idea.

Whatever the future, society's immediate problem is redeployment and re-employment of workers re-engineered out of their jobs. Immediate employment of workers to fill available jobs – and immediate diagnosis and prescription of training to make people employable – will minimize unemployment waiting time and hence underutilized human capacity. A mind is a terrible thing to waste.

Re-engineering is both the fundamental and ultimate tool of change. In its present state, it is helping to adjust business from the old industrial paradigm to a new one of service and information. The concurrent examination of processes, organizations and systems will continue to provide a better understanding of a business's behaviour and its problems. In the future, it will continue to move business from one paradigm to the next. For example, the lines between customer and company (as well as supplier and company) will become blurred as customers are provided with greater access to a company's information and its infrastructure. Who would have considered, even a *few* years ago, that a company such as Federal Express would provide customers with on-line access to its tracking system and real-time delivery status? Guardian Royal Exchange has plans to put its brokers and agents on-line by connecting them to its own computer system.

Our knowledge of technology and how it can make business more productive and enable the creation of new business is sure to change dramatically. The distribution of information is being altered forever by the mass utilization of cellular or other hand-held communications/computing devices which are known nowadays as PDAs (personal digital assistants). Today I travel with the Nokia 9000 Communicator which is a GSM phone operational in about 100 countries worldwide on just one phone number; a messaging device or access terminal enables me to send and receive faxes and access email, browse the worldwide web and enables me to telnet (i.e. connect to other computers); and a palmtop computer–organizer all in one compact package, the size of a spectacle case and at a tenth of the weight of a laptop computer. Devices such as these, unthinkable a year ago, are changing the way people share information, making it easier to provide the process and systems links needed between multiple locations.

As re-engineering is used, it will itself undergo several paradigm shifts as it has since it was popularized by Michael Hammer. Gurus such as Dr Hammer and consulting giants like Booz Allen & Hamilton, Andersen Consulting, Gemini Consulting and CSC Index are already scrambling to re-model their re-engineering vehicles.

Andersen's re-engineering revenue is growing because it is increasingly tying its re-engineering practice to the installation of complex software systems. The managing partner of its Singapore operations hints that a day will come when the name re-engineering may change. Willie Cheng says, 'In the management world, coming out with new terminology and new ways of describing what is essentially the same concept is part of our industry.' Gemini is repackaging its re-engineering offerings and adding strategic-planning work and employee-education programmes.

The firm that started it all, CSC Index, is overhauling its re-engineering practice and may even drop from its lexicon the word it helped make famous. One new model now being tested is 'organizational agility', which stresses the ability to respond rapidly to changes in demand.

James Champy, the consultant who led CSC Index's re-engineering charge, left the firm in 1996 to join Perot Systems Corp, a Dallas computer-services company. From his post in Boston, Champy, too, is broadening his approach. 'There's a need to figure out how to change culture and behaviour more quickly,' he says. He uses 'business transformation' as the working title for his new blend of re-engineering strategy and culture change, but he adds: 'I'd like to find a better label.'

Thomas Davenport, another former Hammer associate, says 'people are starting to realize that changing how people work is more than re-engineering'.

Another big re-engineering player, Booz Allen & Hamilton, thinks it has a better label: 'value engineering'. This new model is the result of a 14-month overhaul that began after a survey of clients discovered that most wanted strategies for growth, not more ways to fire people. 'It focuses more on growth and revenues than traditional business-process redesign,' says Booz Allen senior vice-president Gary Neilson.

All of these changes, these evolutionary and revolutionary steps, will affect both what we do and how we do it. Re-engineering is not just for the 1990s. Rather, it recognizes that all aspects of business systems are forever changing, and that we must challenge ourselves to exchange our current environments for something different, something much better.

The re-engineering revolution profoundly re-arranges the way people conceive of themselves, their work, their place in society. It creates a world in which people have careers rather than jobs, in which they grow rather than get promoted, in which income is based on performance rather than position, colour of their skin or if the CEO likes them. It is a world of fulfilling, exciting, self-actualizing work, but of work that can be stressful and all-consuming. Above all, it is a world of individual responsibility and autonomy, in which both you and your people have the opportunity to exhibit and profit from your individual talents. It's frightening to some people, but in the end you'll find it hard to believe you ever worked in any other way.

Chapter 15
The Asian Way

Many Asian organizations, it has been said, are based on first generation systems and procedures, soaked in second generation perceptions and attitudes, and managed through third generation concepts using fourth generation computers to achieve fifth generation aspirations and longings. Enlightened and progressive Asian CEOs keen to transform that perception have started to ride on the re-engineering wave. They took a while to get there though.

In many ways, Asia is behind the rest of the business world when it comes to applying state-of-the-art management styles. (When Indonesia's T.A. Sutanto took over Bank Dharmala in May 1993, the term re-engineering had yet to waft into Asia's boardrooms and Sutanto himself had not heard of the word 're-engineering' at that time.)

Most Asian organizations are run in top-down fashion, far from the employee empowerment ideal of the re-engineers. They are organized along traditional lines of separate departments with separate functions – R & D, marketing, customer service and so on – rather than around complete processes such as product design. Often Asia's factories are geared to supplying a broad market rather than responding to specific customer needs.

On the face of it, there is much to be done. It took a while for companies here to accept re-engineering, because re-engineering involves asking the fundamental question: 'If the company was started again tomorrow, how would it organize its work?' Very often, the answer is: 'Completely differently', which is a rather onerous reply for management – from *any* part of the world – to receive.

Many of Asia's more progressive companies have since taken the plunge. Scions and heirs taking over the leadership of home-grown business empires from their parents after returning from western universities, equipped with newly acquired MBAs – and with minds open to the benefits of new ideas – have certainly helped pave the way. However, many corporate leaders still have to be persuaded that the rewards of such a shake-up will be worth the effort. At the same time, they are no longer observing with detached amusement the frenetic re-engineering activities of western corporations such as Hewlett Packard, Ford and Citibank because they are aware that those same western companies which have spent the past few years re-engineering are now sleek, efficient and back in expansionary mode. They will soon be challenging Asian companies on their own turf. Tomorrow's most successful Asian corporations will be those who respond to this coming competition before they are forced to.

Is re-engineering in Asia any different?

Hong Kong consultants K.K. Tse and Andros Chan claim that the concept of the Asian way of re-engineering was crystallized during the first ever re-engineering forum held in Hong Kong in early 1995.

At this forum, three companies were invited to share their re-engineering experience: a Hong Kong public utility, a US multinational corporation, and a manufacturing company with a production base inside China.

The representatives from the public utility were the first speakers, followed by the US multinational. The opening remarks made by the representative from the US multinational were most revealing, said Tse and Chan. The speaker has said that learning the experience of the local public utility made him realize that re-engineering the Asian way compared to the US way is as different as a fairytale and a soap opera.

Of course, this is an exaggeration – but there are some elements of truth in it.

The so-called Asian way represents not so much some special inscrutable oriental hocus pocus but more of a modified approach to re-engineering given the unique combination of circumstances in the Asian environment.

First, there is no apparent pressure to downsize for most organizations in Asia, unlike for many firms in the West.

You've probably heard some of those light bulb jokes like how many lawyers does it take to screw in a light bulb? Answer: how many can you afford? OK, how many government employees does it take to change a light bulb in a British National Health Service hospital? The answer is six. That's official and no joke. A study released by the British Audit Commission reported that six people were required to get a light bulb changed, that the task involved 17 different steps and took 20 minutes to organize.

So if the process is re-engineered, the redundant people will probably lose their jobs. Well, in Asia business is booming and people are easily redeployed – a move referred to by James Champy as 'preventive re-engineering'. Employees have their jobs rotated, enlarged, enriched and empowered but the need to 'POP' ('people off payroll', a way of referring to the firing of employees) them is seldom a pressing one. Some companies in the West would need to significantly reduce headcount *regardless* of re-engineering, but most Asian organizations undertaking re-engineering do not have staff reduction as a goal or consequence in re-engineering. Guardian Royal Exchange has been re-engineering its operations in

Asia for about five years now and despite relentless cost cutting this has been accomplished without a single loss of job. The company is now the leading European insurer in Asia with a presence in most Asian capitals.

Of course, concern for traditional assets like cash and property is still there in Asian businesses. But, perhaps because most companies remain family owned and family managed, or stay that way for a long time, focus on people has always been a priority. Asian CEOs tend to look at their organizations as a microcosm of society, not just a place where people come in to work, get paid and then go home, only to return the next day for the same routine. A certain degree of paternalism isn't all that bad. Higashimaru Shoya, a Japanese soy sauce manufacturer, believed that his company could be transformed without 'nuking' or traumatizing the employees and he did just that. In the wake of the agony often rightly or wrongly attributed to re-engineering, it is inspiring to see how companies can replace the fearful spectre of change with a spirit of inspiration and hope.

Most staff involved in or affected by re-engineering initiatives in Asia tend to regard it as an additional opportunity for personal development. Asian workers do not seem to experience the fear, uncertainty, and unrest felt in the West. Middle managers are more flexible and workers less worried about the prospect of unemployment than their counterparts in Europe or the USA. However, to avoid causing undue worries among its staff, Guardian Royal Exchange uses the acronym BPI (business process improvement), says its regional assistant manager for change management and organization development, Avril Gan. In Indonesia, T.A. Sutanto re-engineered Bank Dharmala without once referring to his efforts as 're-engineering'. Of course Sutanto himself and his 'lieutenants' like Ferdinand 'Jojoff' Tan Escobal (who is also his technical adviser, strategic planner and product development chief) know that the bank is re-engineering in a big way but the word 're-engineering' is never used in front of employees.

Asian senior management appear to have a maximum tolerance for criticism, taking criticism as a challenge to apply their leadership skills and as an opportunity to foster participative decision making, thereby creating ownership and buy-in for large-scale organizational change initiatives.

In Asia another significant difference is that companies being re-engineered are usually already market leaders in their fields. In the West, it is often said that there are three types of companies which are embarking on re-engineering: companies in deep trouble; companies not yet in trouble but which soon will be; and companies currently in great shape but which want to create a bigger gap between their competitors and themselves.

Although no hard statistics can be obtained on the actual proportion, it is widely believed that this could be something like 70:20:10 respectively in the early 1990s and changing to 50:30:20 in the last couple of years.

Indeed, Asian organizations undergoing re-engineering, according to Tse and Chan, 'are usually doing very well financially, progressive in outlook, innovative in management approach and are among, or aspiring to be, world-class organizations'. Unlike their western counterparts, they are not plagued by plunging profits.

In Hong Kong, for example, a pioneer in re-engineering has been China & Light Power. In a virtually monopolistic position, they have been one of the bluest of the blue chip companies in the stock market and have been voted by the *Far Eastern Economic Review* as one of the 'most admired' companies in Hong Kong.

Another case in point is the Hospital Authority which is probably the most progressive and best managed public body in Hong Kong. They began re-engineering a few years ago and have now, among all organizations in Hong Kong, the highest proportion of managers who can independently initiate and implement re-engineering projects.

The City University of Hong Kong is yet another example. As a polytechnic-turned-university, the City University is a young institution but it is probably the best among all tertiary institutions in terms of leadership and management. Their effort in re-engineering has been exemplary.

Asian companies also have a better foundation for the launching of re-engineering. Many of these organizations already have in place some form of ongoing improvement programme, or are at least highly quality conscious and customer aware. This enables them to take up re-engineering at a faster pace and be in a position to sustain the effort better than organizations in the West.

While Asian organizations may still operate using traditional management styles, they are more technologically aware and, as with infrastructure, where Asia will eventually build the best because most of the time it is starting from scratch or originating its own innovations, so too with technology – the opportunity to start out fresh is indeed one of Asia's greatest assets. Paris Miki, a Japanese eyewear retailer that has the largest number of eyewear stores in the world, has developed the Mikissimes Design System (also known as the Eye Tailor) which eliminates the customer's needs to review myriad choices when selecting a pair of rimless spectacles – the latest fashion rage. The system takes a digital picture of each consumer's face, analyses its attributes as well as a set of statements submitted by the customer about the kind of look he or she desires, recommends a distinctive lens size and shape, and displays the lenses on the digital image of the consumer's face. The consumer and the optician next collaborate to adjust the shape and size of the lenses until both are pleased with the look. In a similar fashion, consumers select from a number of options for the nose bridge, hinges and arms in order to complete the design. Then they receive a photo-quality picture of themselves with the proposed spectacles. Finally, a technician grinds the lenses and assembles the spectacles in the store in as little as an hour!

Finally, Asian corporations possess what has been termed a twenty-first century perspective. Most Asian organizations undertaking re-engineering do so with a longer view in mind – preparing themselves for the twenty-first century. The implications of such a perspective are manifold.

◆ These organizations are engaging in re-engineering as part of the overall effort to create the twenty-first century organization.

◆ They are not hard pressed to produce short-term results.

◆ The re-engineering initiative is closely tied to the strategic vision of the organization.

◆ Re-engineering is conceived as an important strategic weapon to leapfrog competition and redefine the industry.

◆ Re-engineering is seen as an opportunity to develop intrapreneurs in the organization to compete for the future.

ProData in Singapore, the company started by Singapore's first Novell-certified NetWare engineer Chew Ghim Bok several years ago, is an example of such an organization. Chew started out with a handful of people including his wife, his sister and a cousin. He started to re-engineer processes within his organization long before re-engineering became popular. ProData is now a multi-million dollar organization, having built computer networks for most large Singapore organizations. Chew is poised for growth and is already prepared for the millennium and beyond.

Many Asian organizations currently undergoing re-engineering share this perspective. No wonder some western observers are predicting that Asian organizations may do a better job of re-engineering than their counterparts in the West.

Recommended Reading

Hammer, M. (1990) 'Reengineering work: don't automate, obliterate'. *Harvard Business Review.* Jul/Aug, 68 (4): 104–112.

The pioneering article which started it all. It is inconceivable for someone involved in re-engineering not to read Hammer's work and this journal article is certainly a good place to start.

Hammer, M. and Champy, J. (1993) *Reengineering the Corporation: a Manifesto for Business Revolution* (London: Nicholas Brealey).

While that was the article that started it all, this is the book that has taken the revolution to the fervent pitch it is today. What with various types of operations improvement endeavours mistakenly referred to as re-engineering, and the overnight proliferation of self-professed re-engineering gurus, Hammer's definition of the term and his interpretation of the philosophy of re-engineering is the definitive text to read.

Huber, G.P. (1993) *Organizational Change and Redesign: Ideas and Insights for Improving Managerial Performance* (New York: Oxford University Press).

This book is as practical as Hammer's is philosophical; it complements Hammer's and is well worth a good read as it is rather thought-provoking.

Chapter 1: Positioning for Change

Duck, J.D. (1993) 'Managing change: The art of balancing'. *Harvard Business Review.* Nov/Dec: 109–118.
Useful insights as you prepare your organization to enter into a state of change.

Belasco, J.A. (1990) *Teaching the Elephant to Dance* (London: Random House).
A case history approach to developing new corporate visions and strategies and to empowering people to change.

Kanter, R.M. (1984) *The Change Masters* (London: Allen & Unwin).
Great advice on how to create an environment which allows for participation and innovation.

Chapter 2: Envisioning the Future

Tregoe, B.A., Zimmerman, J.W., Smith, R.A. and Tobia, P.M. (1989) *Vision in Action* (London: Simon & Schuster).
A book touted as 'a book on strategy that's practical . . . the first of its kind.' One client of mine insists that his key executives read this book before embarking on a visioning exercise.

Campbell, A., Devine, M. and Young, D. (1990) *A Sense of Mission* (London: Hutchinson Business Books).
Describes with vivid clarity how world-beating companies have integrated their tough business vision with the values and beliefs of their employees, to create

a unique and enduring source of competitive advantage.

Schein, E.H. (1992) *Organizational Culture and Leadership* (San Francisco: Jossey-Bass).
Schein is widely acclaimed as one of the founders of the field of organizational psychology. In this book, he shows how to identify, nurture and shape the cultures of organizations to achieve their goals and fulfil their missions.

Kotter, J.P. and Heskett, J.L. (1992) *Corporate Culture and Performance* (New York: The Free Press).
Through painstaking research in more than 200 companies, the authors describe how shared values and unwritten rules can profoundly enhance economic success or, conversely, lead to failure to adapt to changing markets and environments.

Kaplan, R.S. and Norton, D.P. (1992) 'The Balanced Scorecard – measures that drive performance'. *Harvard Business Review.* Jan/Feb.
Another pioneering article. This one launched the Balanced Scorecard.

Kaplan, R.S. and Norton, D.P. (1993) 'Putting the Balanced Scorecard to work'. *Harvard Business Review.* Sep/Oct.
A follow-up one year later.

Chapter 3: Using the Balanced Scorecard

Kaplan, R.S. and Norton, D.P. (1996) 'Using the Balanced Scorecard as a strategic management system'. *Harvard Business Review.* Jan/Feb.

A lapse of a few years then this article where you can see the scorecard concept evolving from a measurement tool to a strategic management system.

Kaplan, R.S. and Norton, D.P. (1996) *Translating Strategy into Action: the Balanced Scorecard* (Maidenhead: McGraw-Hill).

At last, the long-awaited book! Here, the authors explain how the Balanced Scorecard can serve as a management system for companies to invest in the long term – in customers, in employees, in new product development and in systems – rather than managing the bottom line to pump up short-term earnings.

Senge, P. (1990) *The Fifth Discipline – The Art and Practice of the Learning Organisation* (New York: Doubleday).

While it is Dutch Shell employee Arie de Geus who is credited with being the originator of the concept of the learning organization, it is American consultant Peter Senge who has introduced it on a wide scale through this landmark book.

Watson, G.H. (1993) *Strategic Benchmarking* (New York: John Wiley & Sons).
As a quality executive with Xerox, Watson has firsthand knowledge of how benchmarking can improve a company's overall performance and competitiveness.

Spendolini, M.J. (1992) *The Benchmarking Book* (New York: AMACOM/The American Management Association).
Benchmarking, looked at from a different angle.

Leibfried, K.H.J. and McNair, C.J. (1992) *Benchmarking: a Tool for Continuous Improvement* (New York: Harper-Collins).
Discusses benchmarking as a continuous improvement approach.

Tucker, F.G., Zivan, S.M. and Camp, R.C. (1987) 'How to measure yourself against the best'. *Harvard Business Review*, Jan/Feb: 8.
Practical advice on benchmarking.

Fuld, L.M. (1985) *Competitor Intelligence: How to Get It – How to Use It* (New York: John Wiley & Sons).
Definitely a how-to guide that points the way.

Chapter 4: Benchmarking Your Way to the Top!

Chapter 5: Operational Diagnosis – Why We Work the Way We Do

Schultheiss, E.E. (1988) *Optimizing the Organization* (Massachusetts: Ballinger Publishing).
A practical approach to organizational effectiveness, long before anyone had heard of re-engineering. Provides an interesting opportunity to look at methodologies which might have been forgotten or have given way to more modern techniques like computer flowcharting, but which are nevertheless still applicable.

Beer, S. (1985) *Diagnosing the System for Organizations* (New York: John Wiley & Sons).
A cleverly written and rather inspiring book for those who are interested in analysing organizational processes and procedures.

Obolensky, N. (1996) *Practical Business Re-engineering* (London: Kogan Page).
Gets to the real roll-up-the-sleeves part of re-engineering.

Chapter 6: Behavioural Analysis – the Touchy Feely Stuff

Woodcock, M. and Francis, D. (1989) *Clarifying Organizational Values* (Aldershot: Gower).
A practical book with how-to advice on understanding, analysing and establishing organizational values.

Woodcock, M. and Francis, D. (1990) *Unblocking Your Organization* (Aldershot: Gower).
Another practical book, loaded with tips and useful suggestions. Some materials in the book are ready for

immediate use. Woodcock and Francis have the ability to discuss organizational and human resource issues in layperson terms and their books are a joy to read.

Woodcock, M. and Francis, D. (1982) *50 Activities for Self-Development* (Aldershot: Gower).
This book is an activity manual to aid in management development. It is packed with ready-to-use forms and checklists. The questionnaire I used for Dow Corning was adapted from one which first appeared here.

Conger, J.A. (1989) *The Charismatic Leader* (San Francisco: Jossey-Bass).
Using illustrations from the careers of charismatic leaders, including Steve Jobs, Lee Iacocca, Mary Kay, John DeLorean, Ross Perot, and others, Conger describes the actual techniques used to motivate others to perform beyond expectations.

Manz, C.C. and Sims, H.P. (1989) *SuperLeadership: Leading Others to Lead Themselves* (New York: Prentice Hall).
In this book, the focus is rather unique: it is on leaders who lead, not for their own glory, not through command and authority, but through a subtle process that leads others to lead themselves to excellence.

Bennis, W. (1989) *On Becoming a Leader* (London: Hutchinson).

Chapter 7: Leadership and Power – Who's Who in Your Organization

A step-by-step guide on acquiring leadership competencies.

**Chapter 8:
A Fish Rots
from the
Head**

Bardwick, J.M. (1991) *Danger in the Comfort Zone* (Maidenhead: McGraw-Hill).
The author shows how the US Department of Defense controls its 134 000 employees through 4 000 laws and 30 000 pages of regulations (including 20 pages on fruit cake and 7 pages on pencils!) and how AT&T's operating procedures manual took up 24 feet of shelf space and devoted 1 200 pages on 'How to properly take an order' and how to put a stop to all that bureaucracy.

Dilenschneider, R.L. (1991) *A Briefing for Leaders* (New York: HarperCollins).
Read all about how executives should manage communication from the peak of the organizational pyramid by creating a vision and a set of corporate values, managing time with an eye towards leaving a legacy, getting support from people, coping with the clutter that clogs today's information pathways, and dealing with the crises and trends that impinge upon business.

Horton, T.R. and Reid, P.C. (1991) *Beyond the Trust Gap* (Illinois: Business One Irwin).
Downsizings, mergers, LBOs and acquisitions have ruptured relations between managers and their employers and created a 'trust gap' that can derail

companies seeking to become more competitive. Here's how to bridge that gap, and more.

Hesselbein, F., Goldsmith, M. and Beckhard, R. (eds) (1996) *The Leader of the Future* (Hemel Hempstead: International Book Distribution).
The editors are all connected with the Peter F. Drucker Institute for Nonprofit Management; they put out a call to their friends, the leading business writers of our day, for their thoughts on the leadership skills necessary to take advantage of the new century's challenges and the result is this book.

O'Toole, J. (1995) *Leading Change* (Hemel Hempstead: International Book Distribution).
'My employees will accept change because I tell them to.' The author shows how that will lead to failure. Change, according to the author, has been and will always be resisted. The only way to overcome that resistance is leadership based on moral values of integrity, trust and an unwavering commitment to doing what's best for your people.

Page, T. (1996) *Diary of a Change Agent* (Aldershot: Gower).
The author is a 40-something management consultant, wrestling with the conflicting demands of a growing business and a growing family. For three years he kept a diary in which he recorded his hopes and fears, his

triumphs and setbacks, his achievements and his mistakes. The diary was originally intended as a way of capturing and reflecting on his experience. It then became clear that by sharing his thoughts with others he could help them to understand the changing work environment and how to operate effectively within it. This honest account will have immediate appeal to anyone serious about business performance improvement, change and learning. But because it deals with the wellsprings of human behaviour its lessons apply far beyond these areas.

Chapter 9 Creativity – Going Where No One Has Gone Before

Rawlinson, J.G. (1981) *Creative Thinking and Brainstorming* (Aldershot: Gower).
A good book to have at your next brainstorming session.

de Bono, E. (1971) *Lateral Thinking for Management: a Handbook* (Maidenhead: McGraw-Hill).
Lateral thinking is considered useful in organization redesign and the author removes the mystique associated with it and treats it as a definite process which can be learned, practised and used.

von Oech, R. (1983) *A Whack on the Side of the Head* (New York: Warner Books).
This is the book to whip out when you are stuck for ideas at the redesign stage. Von Oech identifies ten creative blocks and introduces mind-blowing exercises and activities to help you overcome each block.

von Oech, R. (1986) *A Kick in the Seat of the Pants* (New York: Harper & Row).
In this book, von Oech develops his concepts further.

Morris, D. and Brandon, J. (1993) *Re-engineering your Business* (New York: McGraw-Hill).
Among other useful ideas, this book shows how to design a new organizational structure to position organizations so that they can continually take advantage of changes in the marketplace.

Noer, D.M. (1983) *Healing the Wounds* (San Francisco: Jossey-Bass).
This book is a guide on how to deal with the trauma of workforce transition.

Chapter 10:
Re-engineering and Human Resources – the Minds Behind the Warm Bodies

Petrozzo, D.P. and Stepper, J.C. (1994) *Successful Reengineering* (New York: Van Nostrand Reinhold).
This book provides a heavy focus on implementation, clearly the most difficult aspect of re-engineering.

Goldston, M.R. (1992) *The Turnaround Prescription: Repositioning Troubled Companies* (New York: The Free Press).
A practical and methodological approach to salvaging troubled companies.

Chapter 11:
Redesign – Aiming for the Jugular

Chapter 12: Information Technology as an Enabler

Harwin, R. and Haynes, C. (1991) *Healthy Computing* (Maidenhead: McGraw-Hill).

The book describes the many threats to your health from computers, and the patterns of working that you should change. By following this advice, you will lower your risk of being struck down by those inherent dangers.

Boon, M.E. (1991) *Leadership and the Computer* (California: Prima Publishing).

This book is for people who think for a living. It'll prove just as valuable for those who use computers daily as for those who've never touched a keyboard. Read it to learn innovative ways that computer technology is being applied to business challenges – and how you can join in.

McConnell, V.C. and Koch, K. (1990) *Computerising the Corporation* (New York: Van Nostrand Reinhold).

In many cases, the productivity gains and cost savings promised by IT were lost not because of problems with the system, but because of problems in managing its implementation. This book is not about specific hardware or software applications. It's about helping you see IT in a new light – as a strategic, manageable tool to maximize the potential of your employees and your business, rather than as an element of the business world that seems to have a life of its own.

Gattiker, U.E. (1990) *Technology Management in Organisations* (London: Sage Publications).

Researchers of innovation in organizations frequently distinguish between product and process innovation, the former receiving more attention by firms and more study by researchers. But this book has pointed out that the two types of innovation often occur together.

Walton, R.E. (1989) *Up and Running: Integrating Information Technology and the Organisation* (Maidenhead: McGraw-Hill).
This book reinforces the point that IT cannot change processes by itself, nor is it the only powerful resource. The primary enablers of change in organizations are often organizational/human factors.

Davenport, T.H. (1993) *Process Innovation: Reengineering Work through Information Technology* (Maidenhead: McGraw-Hill).
In this very substantial book, the author shares his wealth of experience as a consultant and business professor at the University of Texas at Austin. A must-read.

Lorenz, C. (1993) 'The very nuts and bolts of change'. *Financial Times*. 22 Jun: 11.

Lorenz, C. (1993) 'The uphill battle against change'. *Financial Times*. 18 Jun: 11.

Lorenz, C. (1993) 'Restoring the order from chaos'.

Chapter 13: Perpetuation – Now and Forever More

Financial Times. 2 May: 11 [case study features Reuters].

Andrews, D.C. and Stalick, S.K. (1994) *Business Reengineering: the Survival Guide* (New York: Prentice Hall).
The book is packed with tools and techniques for those who want to survive and thrive through the chaos and conflict wrought by radical change.

Chapter 14: What Next?

Loh, M. (1990) 'Culture shocks and aftershocks'. *World Executive's Digest.* Jun.
The low-down on how to be successful cross-culturally.

Jamieson, D. and O'Mara, J. (1991) *Managing Workforce 2000* (Hemel Hempstead: International Book Distribution).
The authors first warn of coming catasclysmic demographic changes and then show how to understand these changes and how they'll affect organizations and how to re-energize the commitment of your organization to excellence.

Popcorn, F. (1991) *The Popcorn Report* (London: Doubleday).
How we'll live, what we'll buy, where we'll work – the author, 'the Nostradamus of American Marketing', believes that there's a consumer-driven shake-up coming in the near future that will change the way we live. Although it is marketing-slanted this book makes

excellent reading as it provides information on how to use trends to develop, update and fine-tune your product or service.

Schwartz, P. (1991) *The Art of the Long View* (New York: Doubleday).
The author's message is that you no longer need to hide from the uncertainty that business decisions bring. Though no one knows exactly what the future holds, you can learn to anticipate possible futures and the implications each has for the decisions you make.

Handy, C. (1989) *The Age of Unreason* (London: Business Books).
Charles Handy is the author of four books and teaches at Harvard Business School. He says that organizations, like the frog that can't jump out of the pot in time to save itself, often make changes in a predictable and unfortunate sequence that involves death. He shows you how by challenging the cherished idea that 'we've always done things this way' you can take control of your future.

Ohmae, K. (1990) *The Borderless World* (London: HarperCollins).
Kenichi Ohmae is called upon by executives the world over to help forge strategies in the ever-changing global marketplace. His unique position as an expert in both Japanese and Western business practices permits him to see the merits and drawbacks of each equally well. His

practical experience makes him an invaluable adviser as you hone your strategic vision – a task you must begin now if your company is to prosper in the coming years.

Halberstam, D. (1991) *The Next Century* (New York: William Morrow & Co).
Leaders in a position to shape the future should read this book about how we're now setting the stage for the twenty-first century – and how we can still change the scenery in time for the show.

Bridges, W. (1994) *Jobshift* (London: Nicholas Brealey).
In many companies, jobs are being transformed. Through modern technology and innovative organizational restructuring, companies are creating more efficient, productive ways to organize work. What are the new rules of work? What does the future hold? How can one prepare for it?

McRae, H. (1995) *The World in 2020* (London: Harper Collins).
The author, an award-winning journalist, builds his view of the future by first looking at the world as it is today. He then examines the forces of world change, including demographics, the environment, trade, technology and government.

Heilbroner, R. (1995) *Visions of the Future* (Oxford: Oxford University Press).

What's ahead? Despite the many reasons for unease, Heilbroner is optimistic. In a period when politicians look no further than the next election and we, the electorate, don't look that far, it's inspiring to view with the author far back in history and equally far ahead into the future.

Loh, M. (1996) 'A whole new world'. *World Executive's Digest Technology*. Fall.
If you are 'addicted' to the Internet as I am, you'll understand my fascination for it. This article oozes with excitement about what the Net can offer and will inspire you to believe that it will play an increasingly bigger role in our future.

Collins, J.C. and Porras, J.I. (1994) *Built to Last* (London: Century).
This book is the result of the authors' six-year study of exceptional companies to see what accounts for their success. Collins and Porras surveyed hundreds of CEOs to find out which companies they most esteemed. They chose 18, and then researched them deeply. They charted their growth, analysed their cultures and identified key monuments in their corporate lives.

Dietrich, W.S. (1991) *In the Shadow of the Rising Sun* (Pennsylvania: Penn State Press).
Boiled down, this book's message is this: thanks to a strong central government, its cultural values, and a respected, powerful bureaucracy (best exemplified by

Chapter 15: The Asian Way

MITI, the Ministry of International Trade and Industry), Japan knows exactly where it is and where it's going economically and other countries should take a good hard look at it with a view to learning.

Fucini, J.J. and Fucini, S. (1990) *Working for the Japanese* (Hemel Hempstead: International Book Distribution).
A bit of balance is in order. It becomes clear after reading this book. You'll learn that the much-touted Japanese management methods rest to a large degree on extracting superhuman efforts from employees. But while the Japanese may be willing to sacrifice themselves for the company, most other workers are not. Thus this book will be a cold bucket of water thrown on those who think Japanese methods – at least in their pure form – are the answer to western woes.

Arthur Andersen (1996) *East Meets West: a Survey of Management Culture, Styles and Practices in Asia and the West* (Singapore: The Batey Research & Information Centre).
Do Asia and the West have distinct and separate management styles? The results of this study suggests that they do.

Barlyn, S. (1995) 'It's Singapore!' *Fortune.* 13 Nov.
The magazine asserts that Singapore is the world's number one country for business and explains why.

Index

Achievers 129, 150–51
Action Technologies
  Company 72
Action workflow models
  (organizational
  modelling tool) 72
Active communication 104
  see also Communication
Affiliations of consultants 142
Aimers (concept in
  leadership) 100
American International
  Assurance (corporation)
  31, 32
American Productivity and
  Quality Centre 59
Analysis of benchmarking
  findings 55
Andersen Consulting
  (corporation) 183–4
Anonymity in behavioural
  analysis 77
Application development
  tools 154, 159–60
Asian organizations 187–96
Assembly lines 122–3, 179
Assumptions 131
AT&T (corporation) 57

Baker, James 96
Balanced Scorecard
  measurement system
  43–9
Banking industry 15–16
Behaviour (organizational)
  18, 24
Behavioural analysis 46–7,
  77–87
  anonymity in 77

Beliefs *see* Values
Benchmarking 51–62
  analysis of findings 55
  code of conduct 59
Biotechnology 180–81
Boeing (corporation) 36–7
Booz Allen & Hamilton
  (corporation) xi, 183,
  185
Brainstorming 3, 35–41, 118
British Airways 31
Brown paper system
  explosion
  (organizational
  modelling tool) 74–5
Bureaucracy 19
Bush, George 96
Business activity maps 73
Business process modelling
  66–75

Cascading process in
  communication 40–41, 44
Casey, William 10
Cathay Pacific (airline) 34
Challenging of assumptions
  131
Champy, James 184, 190
Chan, Andros 189
Change 3–19, 23, 24, 25, 28,
  40, 41, 58, 101, 102–3,
  105, 111, 125, 131, 151,
  178, 182, 184
  agents of 79, 103
  management of 25, 169,
  171–3
  resistance to 105, 166–9
  role of information
  technology 153–60

Chaparral Steel
(corporation) 57
Charismatic behaviour 95–7
Cheng, Willie 183–4
Chew, Ghim Bok 196
China & Light Power 193
Chua, Jim Boon 60
Citicorp (corporation) 15–16
City University, Hong Kong
194
Client-server architectures
154, 157–8
Coercive power 99
Collaborative management 89
Comfort group (Singapore
taxi firm) 12–13, 14
Commitment 3, 129
Communication 39, 40–41,
44, 49, 50, 52, 96, 103–5,
106, 129, 183
cascading process 40–41, 44
in benchmarking 55
in information technology
155–6
see also Cascading process
in communication;
Vision statements
Competencies 27, 53, 113
in re-engineering teams
129–30
of consultants 136–44
Competition 19, 29, 196
Competitiveness 27, 30, 52–3,
60, 84
Computerized simulation
models (in operational
analysis) 71
Confidentiality in behavioural
analysis 77
Conflict 164–5
Conformity (to norms) 8–11
Consensus-style management
90

Consultants 17, 130–44
affiliations 142
competencies 136–44
hiring practices 139–40
qualifications 138–9
role of 130–33
selling approach 140
third-party testimonials 142
Consumption of resources 64
Contingency fees (in
consulting) 140
Continuous improvement
programmes 60–61, 169
Continuous learning 51–2
Control factors in operational
processes 64
Copying from other
companies 52
see also Benchmarking
Core competences 27, 53
Cost control 29–30
Creativity 17, 111–19, 129, 148
Credibility 129
Criticism 95
CSC Index (corporation)
183, 184
Customer knowledge (as a
measure) 44, 45
Customer satisfaction 33,
55–7, 60, 62
Customers 45–6, 55–6, 61, 62,
65–6, 147, 166–7

Davenport, Thomas 159, 184
Decision making 17, 29, 40,
73, 83, 84, 90, 96, 107,
131, 135, 148, 149, 150,
168, 192
Delegation 101
Deviance from group norms
8
Diagnosis (in operational
analysis) 63

Digital Equipment
(corporation) 56
Distributed computing
platforms 154–6
Distrust 94
Doing (concept) 94
Dow Corning (corporation)
78–87
Dragons (concept in
leadership) 100
Dysfunction in operational
processes 64, 103, 112,
147

Edison, Thomas 153–4
Efficiency 126
Enthusiasm 3
see also Morale
Entrepreneurship 33, 61, 181
Error rate in operational
processes 65
Escobal, Ferdinand Tan 192
Ethics 40
Etiquette in benchmarking 59
Expectations 102, 178
Expert power 99, 168

Failed product lines 36–7
Fairness 33
Favouritism 94
Feasibility in operational
processes 64
Federal Bureau of
Investigation 92–4
Federal Express
(corporation) 182
Feedback mechanisms 48, 49,
56, 61, 77, 83
Fibre networks 155, 179–80
Finance (as a measure) 44,
46, 47
Flowcharts 67, 73
Focus groups 56, 80, 87

Follow-up of planning
exercises 40–41, 44
Ford, Henry 117
Ford Motor Company 24, 117
Fragmentation 43
Future (planning for) 23–41

Gan, Avril 192
General Electric
(corporation) 18, 57–8
General Motors
(corporation) 17, 89,
150–51
Goal-setting 12, 25, 47
Gordon, William 118
Grace Cocoa (corporation)
34
Group behaviour 5–8
see also Norms (in
organizational
behaviour)
Groupthink (concept) 163
Growth (in organizations) 33
Guardian Royal Exchange 35,
38–40, 182, 190–91, 192

Hammer, Michael 124, 183
Health care 180
Hierarchy chart
(organizational
modelling tool) 70
Honda (corporation) 90
Hong Kong Hospital
Authority 193–4
Hong Leong Group
(Malaysia) 59–60
Hoover, J. Edgar 92–4
Hostility 4
see also Conflict
Human resources (in
organizations) 121–44,
148
Huxley, Aldous 116

IBM (corporation) 37, 90–91, 103
Ideas 16–17, 103, 147
Importance in operational processes 64
Individualized consideration 98
Industrial espionage 58–9
Inertia 105, 168
Information gathering 29
   see also Benchmarking
Information power 99
Information technology 121, 153–60, 179–80, 182–4
Infotainment 180, 181
Initiative 40, 45, 49
Innovation 31, 32, 46, 47, 48, 61, 137
   in information technology 160
Insight 65
Institute of Management Consultants (UK) 143
Intellectual stimulation 98–100
Internal business processes (as a measure) 44, 46
Internal consultants (concept) 90, 91
International Benchmarking Clearinghouse 59
Irwin, Connie 133
Ishikawa diagram (organizational modelling tool) 70
Isolates (in groups) 8

Job descriptions 81, 124, 126, 168
Joyce, James 115–16
Just-In-Time (JIT) 17, 54, 145

Kanban inventory flow management system 54, 57
Kandang Kerbau Hospital (Singapore) 56
Kaplan, Robert 44
Knowledge 16, 18, 27, 36, 65, 103
Kokoro (Japanese concept) 94

Land, Edward 114
Leadership 61, 89–100
   in re-engineering 128, 129
Learning and growth (as a measure) 44, 46
   see also Continuous learning
Learning organizations 14–18
Legitimate power 99
Life cycles of organizations 18–19
Linear programming (organizational modelling tool) 72
Loop-back in operational processes 64
Loyalty 5

Management by exception 98
Management consultants 130–44
Manual functions in operational processes 64
Marriott (hotel group) 32
Mathematical models (organizational modelling tool) 71–2
McDonalds (corporation) 23, 135
McFarlane, Robert 10
McKinsey (consulting firm) 134, 138–9

Mead, Margaret 114
Measurement (as a planning
    tool) 44–9
Miki, Paris 194
Mikissimes Design System 194
Milliken Company 52, 56–7
Misperceptions 80
Mission statements 31–4, 43
Modelling of business
    processes 66–75
Morale 78, 125, 126, 127, 172,
    173
Motivation 40, 81, 82, 85, 95,
    126, 127, 136, 150, 165
Motorola (corporation) xvii,
    52, 56, 171–3
Multi-tasking 146
Multiple data entry in
    operational processes 64

National Bureau of
    Professional
    Management Consultants
    (USA) 143
Network models
    (organizational
    modelling tool) 71
Nithianandan, S. 40–41
Norms (in organizational
    behaviour) 8–12, 18, 77,
    79
North, Lt Col. Oliver 10
Norton, David 44

Ohno, Taiichi 53–4
Openness 130
    in benchmarking 59
Operational analysis 63–75
Opportunities (in SWOT
    analyses) 29–30
Organization charts 70
Organizational culture 3, 5,
    151, 171, 173

Organizational life cycles
    18–19
Osborne, A.F. 118
Outcomes (as a work
    measurement
    parameter) 146
Outside eyes (concept) 131
Ownership (in re-
    engineering) 163, 166

Paradigms (as a predictive
    technique) 13, 145, 177
Paradoxes (as a predictive
    technique) 177
Partnerships 4, 33
Perceptions 80
Performance measurement
    46–7
Perpetuation of a redesign
    163–73
Personal digital assistants 183
Personnel management
    121–2, 124–8
PERT charts 71
Planning 23–41, 44
    for benchmarking 54–5
    for the future 23–41
Power 99–100
Problem solving 61, 78, 90,
    111
Process mapping/modelling
    66–75
Process ownership (in re-
    engineering) 128, 129
ProData (Singapore
    corporation) 196
Productive failure (concept)
    37
Profit 33
Project management 132
Projecting (as a predictive
    technique) 177

Qualifications of consultants
135, 138–9
Quality 39, 52, 60, 61, 62
Questionnaires 78, 79–87

Railway industry 13–14
Re-deployment of workers
181–2
Re-engineering management
structures 128–30
Re-engineering steering
committees 128, 166
Redesign of an organization
112, 145–51
perpetuation of 163–73
Reed, John 15–16
Referent power 99
Relational diagrams
(organizational
modelling tool) 73
Research in benchmarking 55
Resistance to change 105,
166–9
Resource consumption 64
Reuters (corporation) 77–8
Reward power 99
Rework in operational
processes 64
Robots 123, 179
Rock, John 30–31
Roll-down consensus process
see Cascading process in
communication
Rotation of working teams
163–5, 190

Sam, Chong Keen 13
Santayana Review 36
Savings (derived from
consultancy) 140–41
Schultz, George 10
Schwarzkopf, General H.N.
95–6

Sensitivity 129
Shaw, George Bernard 117–18
Shingo, Shigeo 145–6
Shoya, Higashimaru 191
Simulation in operational
processes 67
models 71
Skills upgrading 3–4
Soon Bee, Dr Wan 13
Standards *see* Benchmarking
State transition diagrams
(organizational
modelling tool) 70
Steering committees (in re-
engineering) 128, 129
Stein, Gertrude 117
Strategic Planning Institute's
Council on
Benchmarking (USA) 59
Strengths (in SWOT analyses)
27–8
Suboptimization of effort 43
Sutanto, T.A. 15, 187, 192
SWOT analyses 25–30
Synaptic models
(organizational
modelling tool) 71
Synectics 118
Systems analysis of
operational processes 67

Tan, Beng Cheok 60
Targets 19, 49, 50
Taxi business 12–14
Taylor, Frederick 53
Teamwork 4, 40, 81, 91, 106,
147, 172
conflict 164
in re-engineering 128, 129,
163–5
rotation of teams 163–5
Texas Instruments
(corporation) 58–9

Third-party testimonials (for consultants) 142
Threats (in SWOT analyses) 30
Time factors in operational processes 64
Time saving (in re-engineering) 131–2
Toklas, Alice 117
Tomorrow (concept of) 178
Total Quality Management 17, 32, 52, 107
Training of employees 84, 87, 127, 173, 182
Transactional leadership 98
Transformational leadership 95, 98–9
Tree diagram (organizational modelling tool) 69
Tsars (in re-engineering) 128–9
Tse, K.K. 189

Uncertainty 167, 191
Understanding 65, 66, 106, 115, 117, 130
of operational processes 65–6

Values 24, 33, 40, 105, 151
Vision 19, 24–5, 43–9, 97, 102, 129
implementation of 43
visioning exercises 30–31, 35–41

Vision statements 30–35, 38
follow-up 40–41, 44
glossaries 38–9
guiding principles 39–40

Wan, Soon Bee 13
Warnier-Orr diagram (organizational modelling tool) 69–70
Weaknesses (in SWOT analyses) 28–9
Weinberger, Caspar 10
Welch, Jack 18
Westinghouse (corporation) 52–3
Winograd, Terry 72
Work reorganization 101, 145–51
Workflow software 154, 158–9
Workflows 67–9, 72
Workforce see Human resources (in organizations)
Worthington Steel (corporation) 56
Wuthelam Group (corporation) 31, 33

Xerox (corporation) 37, 51, 56, 58, 93, 111–12, 151

Yoshimura, Masatoshi 114

List of Personnel with Affiliations

Allaire, Paul (Xerox), 151

Buetow, Richard (Motorola), xvii

Cave, David (Dow Corning), 85
Champy, James (Perot Systems), 184, 190
Cheng, Willie (Andersen Consulting), 183–4
Chew Ghim Bok (Prodata), 196
Chin, Steven (Cray Research), 97
Chua, Jim Boon (Hong Leong), 60

Davenport, Thomas (University of Texas), 159, 184

Gan, Avril (GRE), 192
Gerstner, Louis (IBM), 103
Grove, Andy (Intel), 24

Johnson, Kent (Texas Instruments), 58–9

Lautenbach, Ned (IBM), 90
Lynch, James (Sun Microsystems), xvii

Milliken, Roger (Milliken Company), 52, 56–7

Neilson, Gary (Booz Allen & Hamilton), 185
Ng Gak Seng (Pet Computers), 27–30
Nithianandan, S. (Malayan Banking), 40–41

Ohno, Taiichi (Toyota), 53–4

Pearce, Harry (General Motors), 150–51
Puckett, Bernard (IBM), 90–91

Reed, John (Citicorp), 15–16

Sam, Chong Keen (Comfort Group), 13
Shigeo Shingo (Toyota), 145–6
Soon, Bee, Dr Wan (Comfort Group), 13
Sutanto, Titra Adysurya (Bank Dharmala), 15, 187, 192

Tan, Andrew (American International Assurance), 35
Tan, Dr Cheok (Hong Leong), 60

Watson, Thomas (IBM), 37
Welch, Jack (General
    Motors), 18
Wilson, Alan J. (Guardian
    Royal Exchange), 35
Winograd, Terry (Stanford
    University), 72

Company List

Action Technologies
    Company, 72
American Express, 89
American International
    Assurance, 31, 32
Andersen Consulting, 183–4
Arthur D. Little, xi
Asian Development Bank, 14
AT&T, 57

Bank Dharmala, 15
Boeing, 36–7
Booz Allen & Hamilton, xi,
    183, 185
British Airways, 31

Cathay Pacific, 34
Chaparral Steel, 57
Citicorp, 15–16
Comfort, 12–13, 14
Cray Research, 97

Dow Corning, 78–87

Ford Motor Company, 24, 117

Gemini, xi
General Electric, 18, 57–8
General Motors, 17, 89, 150–1
Grace Cocoa, 34
Guardian Royal Exchange,
    35, 38–40, 182, 190–1,
    192

Holiday Inns, 135
Honda, 90
Hong Leong Group, 59–60

IBM, 37, 90–1, 103
Intel, 24

Kandang Kerbau Hospital, 56
Kodak, 89
KPMG Peat Marwick, xi

LL Bean, 51

Malayan Banking, 40–1
Marriott Hotels, 32
McDonald's 23, 135
Milliken Company, 52, 56–7
Motorola, xvii, 52, 56, 171–3

Perot Systems, 184
Pet Computers, 27
ProData, 196

Reuters, 77–8

Sun Microsystems, xvii

Texas Instruments, 58–9
Toyota, xi, 53, 145
TWA, 93

Union Carbide, 74
University of Texas, 159

Walt Disney, 51
Westinghouse, 52–3
William Dunk Partners, 133
Worthington Steel, 56
Wuthelam Group, 31, 33

Xerox, 37, 51, 56, 58, 93,
    111–12, 151

The Management Skills Book

Conor Hannaway and Gabriel Hunt

There is virtually no limit to the skills a manager is expected to use. Some are required every day, others once a month or even once a year. From managing employee performance to chairing meetings, from interviewing staff to making retirement presentations, the list seems endless. How can managers be effective in all these areas? How can they know what to do in every situation?

The Management Skills Book is designed to help all managers facing the challenge of constant change. It is an easy-to-access practical reference work setting out in more than 100 brief guides the elements of the skills needed to succeed as a manager. Each guide is presented in a clear point-by-point style enabling the reader to absorb the key ideas without having to work through a tangle of theory. New and experienced managers alike will welcome the book as a powerful aid to increased effectiveness.

Gower

The New Unblocked Manager

A Practical Guide to Self-Development

Dave Francis and Mike Woodcock

This is unashamedly a self-help book, written for managers and supervisors who wish to improve their effectiveness. In the course of their work with thousands of managers over a long period the authors have discovered twelve potential 'blockages' that stand in the way of managerial competence. They include, for example, negative personal values, low creativity and unclear goals.

By means of a self-evaluation exercise, the reader first identifies the blockages most significant to them. There follows a detailed explanation of each blockage and ideas and materials for tackling the problem.

This is a heavily revised edition of a book that, under its original title, *The Unblocked Manager,* was used by many thousands of managers around the world and appeared in ten languages. The new edition reflects the changed world of management and owes much to the feedback supplied by practising managers. In its enhanced form the book will continue to provide a comprehensive framework for self-directed development.

Gower

The People Side of Project Management

Ralph L Kliem and Irwin S Ludin

This book explains the inter-relationships among the major parties of a project and provides ways for project managers to ensure co-operative, harmonious relationships.

It is written for everyone in business working on a project, regardless of industry. It addresses the psychological and political gaps that affect the outcome of projects. Senior management, project managers, project team members, and clients will all benefit from this book, particularly in mid-size and large firms where the 'people factor' plays an important role. The book will enhance a better understanding of the 'ins and outs' of how major participants of projects think, relate, act and interact.

It identifies the major players in a project environment and discusses the relationships (referred to as the people side) that exist among them from the perspective of the project manager. It discusses the impact of these relationships, throughout the project lifecycle, on major project activities, such as planning, budgeting, change management, and monitoring. It also discusses how project managers can improve these relationships: topics include leading individual team members, motivating the entire team, dealing with the client, and dealing with senior management. Finally, it discusses the qualities of effective project managers that engender co-operative, harmonious relationships among project participants.

Gower

Problem Solving in Groups

Second Edition

Mike Robson

Modern scientific research has demonstrated that groups are likely to
solve problems more effectively than individuals. As most of us knew
already, two heads (or more) are better than one. In organizations it
makes sense to harness the power of the group both to deal with
problems already identified and to generate ideas for enhancing
effectiveness by reducing costs, increasing productivity and the like.

In this revised and updated edition of his successful book, Mike Robson
first introduces the concepts and methods involved. Then, after
setting out the advantages of the group approach, he examines in
detail each of the eight key problem solving techniques. The final
part of the book explains how to present proposed solutions, how to
evaluate results and how to ensure that the group process
runs smoothly.

With its practical tone, its down-to-earth style and lively visuals, this
is a book that will appeal strongly to managers and trainers looking for
ways of improving their organization's and their
department's performance.

Gower

Professional Report Writing

Simon Mort

The ability to write reports that really convince is an invaluable management tool, yet it rarely features amongst the list of skills managers need to be effective. Simon Mort gives that skill the attention it deserves, in the most thorough book on the subject available.

As well as helpful analysis he provides practical guidance on such topics as:

- deciding the format
- structuring a report
- stylistic pitfalls and how to avoid them
- making the most of illustrations
- ensuring a consistent layout

The theme throughout is fitness for purpose, and the text is enriched by a wide variety of examples drawn from business, industry and government. The annotated bibliography includes a review of the leading dictionaries and reference books. Simon Mort's book is an indispensable reference work for managers, civil servants, local government officers, consultants and professionals of every kind.

Gower

Project Leadership

Second Edition

Wendy Briner, Colin Hastings and Michael Geddes

The bestselling first edition of this book broke new ground by focusing on the leadership aspects of project management rather than the technical. This radically revised edition is substantially reorganized, to introduce much new material and experience and bring the applications up to date.

Project leaders now exist in many different types of organizations, and they and their projects extend far wider than the construction work where traditional project management began. This new edition begins by explaining why the project way of working has been so widely and enthusiastically adopted, and provides new material on the role and key competences of project leaders in a wide range of different organizations. The authors provide invaluable guidance to senior managers struggling to create the context within which project work can thrive as well as be controlled. A new section, 'Preparing the Ground' reflects their increased emphasis on getting projects off to the right start, with new insights into the scoping process designed to ensure all parties agree on objectives. It also demonstrates the importance of understanding the organizational and political factors involved if the project is to succeed in business terms.

Part III shows how to handle the issues that arise at each stage of the project's life including a whole new section on the critical process of project team start up. The final section contains a thought-provoking 'action summary' and a guide to further sources of information and development.

Project leadership and the project way of working has moved on. This book will provide both a conceptual framework and a set of practical tools for all those who find themselves permanently or occasionally in the project leader role, as well as an invaluable guide to setting up and maintaining project activity.

Gower

Right First Time
Using Quality Control for Profit

Frank Price

This remarkable book combines simplicity of treatment with depth of coverage and is written in a refreshingly original style. Dispelling the mystique which so often surrounds the subject, and without indulging in complex mathematics, the author explains how to achieve low scrap rates, zero customer rejections and the many other benefits of systematic quality control.

The twin themes of the book are the need for quality to be an integral part of the manufacturing process and the importance of commitment throughout the workforce. Thus it deals not only with QC concepts and techniques but also with the human and corporate relationships whose effects can be critical.

Gower

Why Your Corporate Culture Change Isn't Working...

And What to Do About It

Michael Ward

80% of all change programmes fail.   This book tells you why - and how the other 20% succeed.

Change is risk, yet most organizations today face radical change in order to survive. Markets expand and contract, technology revolutionizes whole industries, companies merge, are taken over, go public, or go back to being private.

Michael Ward has heard the same comments, and seen the same reasons for success or failure in a wide variety of companies, and reflects this experience in the fictitious case studies that form the core of this provocative book. Each follows the same pattern of short narrative, discussion, key points, and concluding principles. Painfully realistic, all managers will wince as they read scenarios that are all too familiar. This is not a book of theory. It is rooted in real experience which will significantly increase the chance of your change programme succeeding.

Gower